ETHNIC CHRONOLOGY SERIES
NUMBER 4

The Italians in America

1492-1972

A Chronology & Fact Book

Compiled and edited by

Reverend Anthony F. LoGatto

1972
OCEANA PUBLICATIONS, INC.
DOBBS FERRY, NEW YORK

242816

Library of Congress Cataloging in Publication Data

LoGatto, Anthony F   comp.
    The Italians in America, 1492-1972.

    (Ethnic chronology series, no. 4)
    Bibliography: p.
    1. Italians in the United States. I. Title.
II. Series.
E184.I8L7   973'.04'51   72-7427
ISBN 0-379-00503-4

Manufactured in the United States of America

TABLE OF CONTENTS

FOREWORD

The melting pot image of America was the product of its time. Today, the very idea is not only non-acceptable but is a disservice to our immigrant fathers whose painful progress constitutes our American heritage. The evolution from attitudes of disdain for unwanted, undesirable minorities to the valued appreciation of nationality and cultural origin, is one of the chief glories of these United States. Indeed, the "unmeltable ethnics" of America are its very fabric. There is only a steady and unbroken stream of ethnics emerging from the Santa Maria of Columbus and the Spanish caravels and the Mayflower, to the Raffaello, the Queen Elizabeth II, and the roaring 747's.

This little volume is the story of one of those groups - the Italians, who came, who went, who stayed, their children and their children's children. It would be a violence to America to imagine it stripped of the rich, warm and varied contribution of the Italians; (so too, of course, were it stripped of any other of its ethnic strains). But no need to do that. Italians and others are here to stay. The real task is to grow, not so much numerically, but as further expression of a people conceived in liberty, nurtured at the breast of rich natural and developed resources, in turn enriching it even more, ready for the next group, hungry for freedom.

The distinctive feature of the Ethnic Chronology Series, incorporating documents as one of its parts, is a tribute to the educational sense (if not genius) of its publishers and editors. American education has suffered from second and third hand sources. Now a student may pick up and read the actual charter of Ferdinand and Isabella of Spain to Columbus setting forth, in detail, the nature and extent of his commission, and his rewards for which he carefully bargained. So too, for so many other historical happenings of interest to students of American history.

The writer deems it a privilege to be involved in this series, so significant in its potential for greater understanding among the people of these United States, indeed, perhaps, of this planet.

1492   Christopher Columbus left the port of Palos, Spain, on
August 3rd; after long, uncertain days and nights, he
sighted the Island of San Salvador (one of the Caribbean
islands), the date being October 12th, 1492. Columbus
was attempting a new route - by sea rather than by land,
to the West rather than to the East - to the rich markets of
India and China. In fact, Columbus carried with him a
letter from King Ferdinand of Spain to his "Royal Brother,"
the Emperor of China.

1493   Christopher Columbus, realizing that his progress to the
Orient had been interrupted by an unchartered landmass,
made three other voyages to the new world, all in an attempt to by-pass the landmass and reach the East. The
dates of the later voyages were 1493, 1498 and 1502.

1496   John Cabot (Giovanni Caboto), an Italian, probably of Genoa,
received from King Henry VII, of England, on March 5,
1496, Letters-Patent to find a short, high-latitude route to
the Orient for trade purposes but especially for spices, such
as pepper, cloves and nutmeg, necessities in days of no
refrigeration. Henry had turned down Columbus' request;
he was not going to lose this opportunity for a faster, northern route to the land of trade and take title to lands that
might be discovered.

1497   Cabot set out from Bristol, England, where he had settled
with prosperous merchants of that fabulous provincial
port. The date was about May 20, 1497. The actual
point of departure was Dursey Head, Ireland, about May
22nd. He made a landfall at New Foundland, June 24th,
a voyage of only 32 or 33 days from Ireland. Henry VII
referred to it as the "new founde lande" which became
Newfoundland. As for Cabot, he thought he reached a
new isle, off the Eurasian continent and that he had hit
upon the passage to the "Cathay."

1497   Amerigo Vespucci, a noble Florentine, was sent by the
Bank of the Medici to Spain where he helped to outfit the
ships for Columbus' second voyage in 1493. Vespucci
made four voyages himself to the new world, the first two
under the flags of Spain, in 1497 and 1499, the last two for
Portugal in 1501 and 1503. (It seems some doubt exists
about the first voyage). In the course of these voyages,

Vespucci followed the coastline of South America, made maps and astronomical observations such as to estimate the circumference of the earth which he did with amazing accuracy. He also noted, for the first time, that the new land was a continent, not many small islands. These descriptions were so numerous and popular, so the story goes, that a German mapmaker, publishing the writings of Vespucci, said "Now a fourth part (of the world) has been found by Amerigo Vespucci, and I do not see why we should be prevented from calling it Amerige or America." Thus the name of America.

1498   On February 3, Henry VII issued Letters-Patent to his "beloved John Kaboto" for a second voyage. The trip began about the beginning of May, 1498. Five ships set out, fully furnished and manned. One of them turned back in distress to Ireland shortly after. The other four ships and Cabot never returned and were never heard from again. Like Columbus, John Cabot died without awareness of the vastness, and the significance of his discoveries.

1506   Christopher Columbus died a very much saddened and disappointed man. S. E. Morison records a wry observation: "As a literary wit remarked, America was discovered by accident, not wanted when found, and early explorations were directed to finding a way through or around it."

1519   Antonio Pigafetta, an Italian gentleman, accompanied Ferdinand Magellan, who set out in September, 1519, from the Spanish port of San Lucar de Barrameda, to reach the Moluccas or Spice Island for the purposes of trade, Pigafetta's manuscript is one of the most important geographical documents in existence. He was a sharp observer and a scrupulous recorder who wrote as he saw history unfold. He recorded flora and fauna; manners, customs and languages; and he accurately described lands and seas never seen by Europeans before. Man's first voyage around the globe by a sailing vessel, for so it turned out to be, was more astonishing to the folk of 1522 than the orbiting of the earth by the first satellite in 1957.

1524   Giovanni Verrazzano, a Florentine explorer and humanist, was the first European to sail into New York Bay, record its exact position on a map, and give it a name, Angouleme, the family name of Francis I, King of France, under whose flag he sailed.

Like Columbus and his other predecessors, Verrazzano set out for the new world with the same purpose in mind. "My intention on this voyage was to reach Cathay and the extreme eastern coast of Asia, but I did not expect to find such an obstacle of new land as I have found; and if for some reason I did expect to find it, I estimated there would be some strait to get through to the Eastern Ocean." (the Pacific Ocean).

1524   Verazzano's letter to Francis I, his official report of his discoveries, is a classic and a landmark in history.   Like the narrative of Columbus, the report is first-hand, personal documentation on the exploration and description of the Atlantic coast of the United States and Canada - from the Carolinas to Newfoundland.   The narrative is rich in detail of animals, trees, grasses and wild flowers and a vivid eye-witness account of the American Indians.   It is the earliest geographical, typographical and ethnological survey of the previously undescribed coastline from Florida to New Foundland.

1539   Friar Marco Da Nizza travelled the border of a desert, now known as the southern boundary of Arizona; crossing the desert he reached what is now the Gila Valley; and from the valley he touched the present region of Phoenix, Arizona.

1639   Peter Caesar Alberto is described in the historical archives of Kings County (New York) as "the Italian."   He is regarded as the first Italian to reside in Brooklyn, then known as New Amsterdam.   There is persuasive evidence that he later developed a large tobacco plantation in Wallabout Bay.

1678   Henri de Tonti, "The Man with the Iron Hand", arrived in America to serve with La Salle, the famous explorer, whose great aspiration it was to travel the full length of the Mississippi River from the Great Lakes down to the Gulf of Mexico and claim it all for the King of France.   To pay for this venture, the fur trade had to be exploited to the full, and means of transportation had to be devised.   Thus, Tonti built the first crude sailing vessel to sail on the Great Lakes.

1682   Henri de Tonti and La Salle, after torturous travel and heartbreaking hardships, explored the entire length of the Mississippi River to its delta where it empties into the Gulf of Mexico.   They took possession in the name of

Louis, King of France, and named the southern section "Louisiana," after the King.

1686   Henri de Tonti built a fort and set up a trading post at the Arkansas River, the first European settlement in the State. Hence, Tonti is sometimes called the "father of Arkansas," and the Arkansas River was known for a while as La Riviere de Tonti (Tonti's River).

1702   Father Eusebio Francesco Kino (Chino), explorer, missionary, rancher and historian. As an explorer he proved that California is a peninsula and not an island. His minute exploration and mapping of lower California and the whole of Pimeria included the southern part of the State of Arizona. Father Chino travelled more than 20,000 miles, very often opening trails that had never been trod by a white man before. As a missionary he built more than thirty churches and chapels and baptized more than 4,500 persons. Father Chino recorded and drew maps of his work and explorations. His Favores Celestiales is a valuable and autobiographical chronicle.

1736   Onorio Razzolini is regarded as the first Italian to hold public office in America; was appointed Armourer and Keeper of the Stores of Maryland.

1773   Philip Mazzei arrived in Virginia. His revolutionary spirit and strong ideals of democracy quickly bound him by hoops of steel to Jefferson. Mazzei and Jefferson collaborated on a series of articles espousing political freedom. Mazzei's profound statement that "All men are by nature equally free and independent. This equality is essential to the establishment of a liberal government . . . . A truly republican form of government cannot exist except where all men - from the very rich to the very poor - are perfectly equal in natural rights" was the fierce conviction shared by Jefferson and Mazzei and was reflected in so much of the American Constitutional theory. Mazzei's agricultural experimentation and introduction of new strains of flowers, fruits and vegetables produced new eating patterns. Jefferson, a horticulturalist in his own right, admired Mazzei's skills and abilities with the soil. He was so impressed with the qualities of Mazzei's workers that he proposed expanded immigration from Italy.

1774   Giuseppe Maria Francesco Vigo, frontiersman and hero of the American Revolution, arrived in New Orleans, Louisiana, from Italy. Vigo was a shrewd fur trader whose wealth and knowledge of the forest trails and the Indian tribes substantially contributed to the conquest of the Northwest Territory. His financial contribution was so exhaustive that he died impoverished. Many years later the United States Supreme Court acknowledged $49,898.60 as conpensation to his heirs for his contribution to the war. It was no measure, however, of his fierce patriotism and his giving of himself.

1774   Nicholas Biferi established a music school and dance school for young ladies, possibly the first of its kind on this continent. He was a noted harpsichordist and gave recitals in New York.

1776   William Paca, as a member of the Continental Congress, signed the American Declaration of Independence, thus cutting off the American colonies from Mother England. Prior to this, Paca had served in the Maryland legislature.

1776   William Paca was elected one of fifteen members of the first Maryland State Senate.

1778   William Paca was appointed Judge of the General Court of Maryland.

1778   Carlo Bellini, as Professor of Romance Languages at William and Mary College, was the first Italian professor in the United States. He was a friend of Jefferson and Mazzei.

1779   Giuseppe Maria Francesco Vigo took Fort Vincennes in the most critical and strategic struggle for the Northwest Territory.

1780   William Paca was appointed by Congress Chief Justice of the Court of Appeals in Admiralty and Prize Cases.

1782   William Paca was elected Governor of Maryland and served three terms, from 1782 to 1785.

1789   William Paca was appointed Judge of the Federal District Court by President George Washington.

1789   Giuseppe Maria Francesco Vigo was consulted by General George Washington for the defense of the West. County Vigo in Indiana was so named to commemorate his service to his adopted land.

1791   Alessandro Malaspina headed a scientific expedition, surveying the Pacific coast from Alaska to Mexico.

1800   Paolo Busti arrived in America from Milan, Italy, and took up active management of the Holland Land Company. Through Busti's skillful planning and developing, five million acres of land evolved into American villages, towns and cities.

1801   Father Charles Constantine Pise was the first priest born in America (State of Maryland) of Italian extraction.

1805   Thomas Jefferson recruited fourteen musicians from Italy to form the nucleus of the famous United States Marine Band. Six Italian conductors graced the band in its long history: Carusi, Pulizzi, Pons, Lucchesi, Scala and Fanciulli.

1805   Lorenzo Da Ponte, of Italian-Jewish ancestry, came to America at age 56. Father Da Ponte was a priest, linguist and musician. He became the first teacher of Italian in New York City in 1806; and in 1825 he received an appointment as the first professor of the Italian language and literature at Columbia College (now Columbia University) without benefit of any stipend. Da Ponte also wrote libretti for several of Mozart's operas.

1815   An Act of Congress raised Georgetown College to the rank of University, thus making it the first Catholic University in the United States. Father John Grassi was its first president.

1819   Charles Botta wrote the first history of the American Revolution in Italian. A four volume work, it was translated in 1834, under the title of A History of the War of Independence by Nathan Whiting, New Haven, Connecticut.

1825   Barber of Seville the first Italian opera to be sung at the Park Theatre in New York City.

1827   Father Joseph Rosati was appointed first Bishop of the newly created diocese of St. Louis, Missouri. He is also responsible for the first hospital and orphan asylum in the Middle West. A school for deaf-mutes is said to have been the first of its kind in the country.

1829   Father Charles Constantine Pise wrote the first Catholic novel entitled: Father Rowland, A North American Tale. He wrote other novels and his poem, "Flag of my Native Land," is still well known.

1832   Father Charles Constantine Pise was the first and only Catholic Chaplain of the Congress of the United States. He was made a Knight of the Holy Roman Empire and the first American priest to be invested as a Knight of the Sacred Palace and Count Palatine.

1833   Father Samuel Mazzuchelli, educator, architect, philologist, wrote a book of prayers in the Winnebago language. It is said to be the first work in any Sioux language ever published.

1835   Antonio Meucci, alleged to be the true inventor of the telephone, arrived in Cuba from Italy to become Superintendent of Mechanism and Scenic Designer of the Tacon Theatre. (He was a mechanical engineer). While experimenting with electricity, by sheer chance, he heard a voice transmitted through an electric wire. To be near a source of technical equipment he moved to New York in 1850.

1837   John Phinizy probably was the first son of an Italian immigrant (Ferdinando Finizzi) to serve as Mayor of an American city, Augusta, Georgia.

1838   Philip Traetta, musician and composer from Venice, a friend of Presidents Madison and Monroe, established a conservatory of music in Boston, Massachusetts, and later established a second one in Philadelphia, Pennsylvania. He composed several musical works and was the author of An Introduction to the Art and Science of Music (1829) and Vocal Exercises and Rudiments of the Art of Singing, 2 vols. (1841-43).

1839   Charles Del Vecchio became New York City's first Italian-American Fire Commissioner.

1840   Father Samuel Mazzuchelli built the first Catholic churches in both Iowa and Wisconsin.

1846   Salvatore Catalano was a sailing master in the United States Navy until his death in 1846. He piloted "Old Ironsides."

1847   Astor Place Opera House, New York City, was built especially for Italian Opera.

1850   Giuseppe Garibaldi arrived in New York as a political refugee. He lived with Antonio Meucci in Rosebank, Staten island. They eked out a living by hunting, fishing and making candles.

1850   An Italian consulate was opened in San Francisco, California, headed by Colonel Leonetto Cipriani, to care for Italians on the West Coast.

1851   Santa Clara College in California was founded by the Italian Jesuit, Father Giovanni Nobili.

1851   Father Gregorio Mengarini, Roman missionary and educator, was Treasurer at the College of Santa Clara in California, the first collegiate institution on the Pacific Coast.

1853   Father Benedict Sestini, astronomer and mathematician, made a series of drawings of the sun's surface, which were engraved and published (44 plates) as "Appendix A" of the Naval Observatory.
Author: Analytical Geometry, (1852) and Elements of Geometry and Trigonometry (1860).

1854   The New York Academy of Music opened on Fourteenth Street at Third Avenue in Manhattan, New York. Here opera found a permanent home and during its brilliant existence it hosted the most gifted artists of the day. Its inadequacy of size made imperative the Metropolitan Opera House in 1883.

1855   Constantino Brumidi, the "Michelangelo of the United States Capitol," was employed by the Superintendent of the Capitol, Captain Montgomery C. Meigs, to decorate the Agriculture Committee room. This was the first example of fresco in America. Indeed, Brumidi's work was so magnificient, that he was retained for the remainder of his life, a period of twenty-five years. During that time he decorated practically every important area of the Capitol from the various rooms and chambers to the Capitol rotunda containing a frescoed frieze of fifteen historical groupings and capped by the huge frescoed canopy in the eye of the Capitol dome, measuring 4,664 square feet of fresco. A tragic near fall while working on the high scaffolding up in the rotunda terminated his work. He died shortly thereafter in 1880. Brumidi had come to America as a political exile. Here he found refuge and freedom. His gratitude was expressed eloquently: "I no longer have any desire for fame or fortune. My one ambition and my daily prayer is that I may live long enough to make beautiful the Capitol of the one country on earth in which there is liberty."

1859   Emanuel Smith, grandfather of Alfred E. Smith (the famous
            former Governor of New York and candidate for the Presi-
            dency in 1928) died in New York City on April 10th. An
            official letter of the Municipal Archives and Record Center
            of the City of New York certifies Italy as his birthplace.
            How he acquired the surname of "Smith" is not clear. It
            may be another instance of a change of name for conven-
            ience or an anglicization by immigration officers - a not
            unusual occurence in those days.

1859   St. Anthony of Padua Roman Catholic Church, (located on
            Sullivan Street, New York City) was founded by the Fran-
            ciscan Fathers to serve the Italian immigrants living in
            the lower Manhattan district. It is a well known landmark
            which still attracts thousands of visitors.

1860   Antonio Meucci gave a public demonstration to a group of
            people who actually heard "La Marseillaise" over a wire at
            a considerable distance from its source. Meucci, unfor-
            tunately, was plagued with hard luck, bad friends, accidents,
            betrayals, etc. Unable to raise the money for the legal
            work to procure a patent on his "telephone", he settled
            for a "caveat" in 1871. (Caveat gives notice of the inven-
            tion and precludes others from filing for the same idea).

1860   Father Gennaro De Concilio arrived in America. He was
            a Professor of Logic at Seton Hall University in South
            Orange, New Jersey. He wrote the famous Baltimore
            Catechism used for fifty years, without revision, through-
            out the United States.

1861   Giuseppe Garibaldi was offered a commission as Major
            General in the Union Army by President Abraham Lincoln.

1861   Luigi Palma Di Cesnola, born in Italy, served in the Civil
            War and rose to the rank of Colonel. President Lincoln
            had given an oral committment to raise Cesnola to the rank
            of general, but Lincoln's tragic death intervened. His
            real fame, however, came as an archaeologist, in which
            science he was a pioneer. On the strength of this he was
            made the first director of the Metropolitan Museum of Art
            in New York City. It was his collection of Cyprian antiques
            that formed a large part of the exhibit in the early years of
            the Museum.

1861   Gaetano Lanza founded the Massachusetts Institute of Tech-
            nology and for twenty-nine years was head of the Depart-
            ment of Mechanical Engineering.

1866   Father Benedict Sestini founded the Messenger of the Sacred Heart, a Catholic magazine, with the largest circulation in the world; he was its editor from 1866 to 1881.

1869   Father Joseph Neri perfected "an electrical lighting system for exhibition and lecture purposes in which he used carbon electric lights.   In pursuing his investigations he first used large batteries, then magneto machines and finally dynamos."

1869   Father Angelo M. Paresce conceived and erected the College of the Sacred Heart at Woodstock, Maryland.

1870   Carlo Antonio Rapallo, a New York lawyer, was elected to the Court of Appeals of the State of New York and served with distinction until his death in 1887.

1870   Dr. Giovanni Ceccarini was the first Chairman of the Sanitary Committee of the Department of Health of the City of New York.   He was a most distinguished physician and generally regarded as second to none among the most renowned physicians and surgeons of America.

1870   Ignazio Persico was consecrated Bishop of the Diocese of Savannah, Georgia.

1872   Antonio Meucci tried to interest New York District Telegraph (branch of Western Union) in making an experimental trial of his telephone on their wires.   They accepted his models and papers, but they gave him one excuse after the other for over two years.   When in disgust he asked for his models, they simply stated they had lost them. In 1876, Alexander Graham Bell filed for the same idea. Meucci appealed to the Patent Office in Washington, D. C. The answer: all papers related to the "Speaking Telegraph" had disappeared from the file.

1872   Alfred Emanuel Smith, an Italian, father of "Al" Smith, married Catherine Mulvehill.   "Al" Smith was born of this marriage on December 30, 1873.   Exactly two years later, his sister, Mary, was born.   It was Mary who gave the information about her Italian father and grandfather to Frances Perkins, former Secretary of Labor under President Franklin D. Roosevelt, when Miss Perkins was writing a biography of Governor Smith.

1872   Father Pietro Bandini is best known by Italian-Americans

of the Bank of Italy in California. It is now called the Bank of America, the largest banking institution in the world.

1905   Charles J. Bonaparte served as Secretary of the Navy under President Theodore Roosevelt.

1906   Charles J. Bonaparte was appointed Attorney General by President Theodore Roosevelt.

1906   Amedeo Obici, businessman, was the founder of the "Planters Peanuts" enterprises in Virginia. He is known as the Peanut King of America.

1906   Mama Leone Restaurant opened in New York City. Today, some four thousand people eat there daily.

1908   Charles J. Bonaparte founded the Federal Bureau of Investigation (The FBI). He died in 1921.

1908   Arturo Toscanini, of La Scala fame, opened the 1908 season of the Metropolitan Opera House on November 16th with Aida. The response was overwhelming. His career literally boomed and skyrocketted. His preeminence as a conductor was established practically without competition.

1908   Giulio Gatti-Casazza (from La Scala in Milan, Italy) became general manager of the Metropolitan Opera Company and remained director until retirement in 1934. He introduced 110 works novel to the Metropolitan.

1910   Giacomo Puccini visited America for the world premiere of his opera - La Fanciulla Del West (The Girl of the Golden West) on December 10th.

1913   Anthony Caminetti was appointed Commissioner General of Immigration by President Woodrow Wilson.

1913   Angelo Patri, first Italian born educator to become a school principal in the United States. (Public-School 145, Bronx, New York).

1913   Rudolph Valentino came to America. He became a world renowned screen star of the silent movies and the idol of literally millions of women. He starred in The Sheik; Camille; Blood and Sand and numerous other films.

1915   Father Nicola Fusco co-founded the magazine "Il Carroccio." He was also an editor-writer for the national weekly newspaper "Il Crociato," for many years; and wrote several books including <u>Life of Christ</u>, acclaimed both in America and Italy.

1915　Il Caroccio, published in New York City from 1915 to 1935, a monthly bi-lingual cultural magazine dealing with social and political problems of Italian Americans in America, was co-founded by Agostino De Biasi.

1916　Fiorello H. La Guardia, born in New York City of Italian Jewish parentage, became a member of Congress, as Representative from the 14th Congressional District of Manhattan and was re-elected in 1918 while in active service in the Air Force. He re-entered Congress in 1922 as Representative from the 20th Congressional District, where he remained until 1932. La Guardia was champion on the floor of Congress fighting for the peasant masses of his City. He fought the quota (immigration) system as bigoted. With him, some say, Italian Americans came of political age.

1916　Giovanni Schiavo came to America from his native Italy. He probably did more to promote the Italian name than any other single person. His volumes speak for themselves: <u>Italians in Chicago</u>, 1928; <u>Italians in Missouri,</u> 1929; <u>Italians in America before the Civil War</u>, 1934; <u>Italian-American History</u>, 2 vols, 1947 and 1949.

1917　American immigration policy began to evolve with the passage of the literacy test law. Though on its face a quality test, it was in reality the first legal step toward a restrictive and selective policy as applied to Europeans. It favored the northern western nordic groups and limited the southern and eastern European peoples not considered as desirable.

1921　After World War I, Congress hurriedly passed a new frankly restrictive law based on the principle of ethnic quotas. It limited immigrants of each nationality to 3% of the number of that nationality resident in the United States according to the census of 1910; and cut the total annual number of quota aliens to 357,000. The majority of immigrants from south-eastern Europe came too late to be recorded in the 1910 census. This was admittedly a discriminatory

and 1948. Twice Batting Champion of the American League, 1939, 1940. Voted Most Valuable Player three times: 1939, 1941, and 1947. Elected to the National Baseball Hall of Fame in 1955. Autobiography: Lucky to Be a Yankee, 1946.

1936   George Speri Sperti, scientist, was one of the six illustrious Americans honored by Pope Pius XI at the Pontifical Academy of Science. He invented the Sperti Sun Lamp, the K-Va Meter, a light treatment process and the famous healing ointment known as Sperti's biodyne.

1937   Arturo Toscanini conducted the NBC Symphony Orchestra until 1954, at which time his farewell performance produced a sensational outburst of admiration, joy and sorrow.

1938   Enrico Fermi received the Nobel Prize for his experiments with radioactivity. The citation read as follows: "To Enrico Fermi of Rome for his identification of new radioactive elements produced by neutron bombardment and his discovery made in connection with this work, of nuclear reactions effected by slow neutrons."

1939   Enrico Fermi became professor of physics at Columbia University and remained there until 1945. This period was extremely productive for his advances in the development of nuclear fission. He was at that time without doubt the greatest living expert on neutrons.

1939   Charles Poletti was elected Lieutenant Governor of New York State.

1941   Enrico Fermi became involved in the all-out effort to produce the atomic bomb. In 1942 he relocated to Chicago with the rest of the team working on the bomb. In 1943 the operation was moved to Los Alamos in New Mexico. On July 15, 1945, the first atomic bomb was exploded at Alamagordo (White Sands), New Mexico.

1941   Pascal P. Pirone, plant pathologist, invented the Rutgers aero plant propagator. He has long been associated with The New York Botanical Garden, where he presently holds the positions of Senior Plant Pathologist and Senior Curator of Education. He has taught in the departments of plant pathology at Cornell University and Rutgers - The State University. Author: Diseases and Pests of Ornamental Plants, 1970 and several other books on horticultural subjects.

1942   Charles Poletti, Lieutenant Governor of New York State
                became Governor when Herbert Lehman was elected to
                the United States Senate.

1942   Mario Biaggi, born in New York City, the most decorated
                policeman in the United States, served on the New York
                City Police Department from 1942 to 1965.

1942   Peter Sammartino developed Fairleigh Dickinson Univer-
                sity in New Jersey and was its president for more than
                twenty-five years. Author: Of Castles and Colleges,
                1972.

1942   On Columbus Day, President Franklin D. Roosevelt de-
                clared Italians were no longer to be considered enemy
                aliens.

1943   Sergeant John Basilone, World War II Marine hero, was
                the first enlisted Marine in World War II to receive the
                Congressional Medal of Honor. He gave his life for his
                country on the first day of the invasion of Iwo Jima in
                1944. He was awarded the Navy Cross posthumously.
                General MacArthur called him a "one man Army."

1945   John O. Pastore, native of Providence, Rhode Island, was
                elected Governor of that State.

1945   Vincent Impelliteri, born in Italy, was elected President
                of the City Council of New York. He happened to be the
                first Italian-American to get a place on a city-wide
                democratic ticket.

1946   Mother Frances Xavier Cabrini, a United States citizen,
                was canonized a saint by Pope Pius XII.

1948   Paul Peter Rao was appointed Chief Judge of the United
                States Customs Court. He is the only judge of Italian
                background who has served as chief judge of a national
                federal court, i.e., the United States Customs Court.
                He also served as Assistant Attorney General of the
                United States under Presidents Franklin D. Roosevelt and
                Harry S. Truman, 1941 to 1948.

1948   Italian Historical Society of America founded by John La
                Corte to promote and foster the Italian heritage and its
                contributions to American civilization. Mr. La Corte
                was the person most instrumental in having the Narrows
                Span called the Verrazzano Bridge.

1949   Carmine G. De Sapio took over the leadership of New
            York's Tammany Hall, becoming the first Italian Ameri-
            can political boss with national influence.

1950   John O. Pastore, of Rhode Island, was elected United States
            Senator, the highest elective office achieved by anyone of
            Italian lineage.

1950   In this election year four Italo-Americans ran for the
            office of Mayor of the City of New York, Vincent Impelli-
            teri, Ferdinand Pecora, Edward Corsi and Vito Marcanton-
            io. Impelliteri, an Independent, won. He was the second
            Italian American to hold the highest executive position in
            the City of New York.

1950   Dr. Myrtle Cheney Murdock, wife of the Arizona Congress-
            man, found the unmarked grave of Constantino Brumidi,
            painter of the Capitol, in the old Glenwood Cemetery where
            he had been buried and forgotten for 72 years. Her exten-
            sive research culminated in the publication of Constantino
            Brumidi, Michelangelo of the United States Capitol, a beau-
            tifully illustrated and masterfully written volume. It was
            her valiant efforts that led to the marking of the grave
            through an act of Congress, appropriating $400.00 for a
            bronze marker, and that led to the placing of the marble
            bust in the Brumidi corridor.

1951   Juvenal Marchisio, former Judge of the Domestic Relations
            Court of the City of New York, was asked by Cardinal
            Stritch of Chicago and the National Catholic Resettlement
            Council to form and head a nationwide organization - now
            known as the American Committee on Italian Migration
            (ACIM) - which would develop a program devoted to the
            liberalization of United States immigration policies. This
            Committee has grown into a network of about 127 Chapters
            throughout the country and is most effective in the passage
            of immigration legislation.

1952   Rocco A. Petrone was Development Officer at Redstone
            Missile Development Center at Huntsville, Alabama, from
            1952 to 1955. Became Manager of the Apollo Program
            at Kennedy Space Center from 1960 to 1966, then Director
            of Launch Operations from 1966 to 1969. He was advanced
            to Apollo Program Director, NASA, from 1969 to date.
            Colonel Petrone gave the briefing when President John F.
            Kennedy and Vice-President Lyndon B. Johnson visited the
            Space Center in 1962.

1952   John J. Muccio was appointed Ambassador Extraordinary
              to Korea.   Prior to that time, at the end of World War II,
              he served as political advisor to the Supreme Allied Com-
              mand in Germany.

1952   Roberto Vaglio-Laurin, engineer, came to the United States,
              and is esteemed as one of the world authorities in hyper-
              sonics.   He is Professor of Aeronautics and Astronautics
              at New York University.

1952   Rocky Marciano, born in Brockton, Massachusetts, won
              the Heavyweight Championship Title on September 23rd,
              when he knocked out Jersey Joe Walcott.   Rocky never lost
              a pro fight at any time; he defended his title six times and
              retired undefeated on April 27, 1956.

1953   Frank Sinatra, Sr., singer and actor, received the Academy
              award for supporting actor for his role in the film "From
              Here to Eternity," as well as many other notable awards.
              He also wrote the lyrics for the popular song "This Love
              of Mine."

1954   Enrico Fermi died at age 53.   Samuel K. Allison said of
              him: "Enrico was one of the most brilliant intellects of
              our century.   Here was a man who possessed a most ex-
              traordinary endowment of the highest human capabilities."

1955   Eddie Arcaro, a leading horse jockey, was elected to the
              Hall of Fame.

1956   Alberto D. Rosselini was elected Governor of the State of
              Washington.

1956   John J. Marchi was elected to the New York Senate.   In
              1969 he was the candidate of the Republican and Conserva-
              tive parties for the office of Mayor of the City of New York.

1956   Foster Furcolo, a liberal Democrat, was elected Governor
              of the State of Massachusetts.

1956   Perry Como, popular entertainer, received the Emmy
              Award for Best Personality.   His gentle and wholesome
              attitudes have earned for him the esteem and respect of
              his colleagues in the entertainment field and of the general
              public.

1958   Michael V. Di Salle was elected Governor of the State of
              Ohio.

1959   Joseph F. Carlino was the first Italian American to serve
                as Speaker of the New York State Assembly.   He held that
                post until 1964.

1959   Emilio Segrè, physicist, was awarded the Nobel Prize.   He
                was a pupil, close friend and collaborator with Enrico
                Fermi during most of Fermi's active years as a scientist.
                Author: Enrico Fermi, Physicist, 1970.

1961   John Anthony Volpe was elected Governor of the State of
                Massachusetts and re-elected in 1965.

1961   The Mutual Educational and Cultural Exchange Act was
                enacted.   This law promoted cultural and educational
                programs with every country in the world.   As it affected
                the Italians in America, however, during its first seven
                years of existence, the Act appropriated grants to 1,660
                Italian students, teachers, specialists, lecturers and re-
                search scholars to come to the United States.   For the
                same period, 1,470 American students, teachers, lecturers,
                researchers and specialists received grants to go to Italy.
                This was one of a multitude of cultural exchanges effected
                under the Act.

1961   Dominic Coscia, born in Brooklyn, New York, was ordained
                a Franciscan friar in 1949.   In 1961 he was consecrated as
                Bishop of Jolai, Brazil.

1962   Anthony Celebrezze was appointed by President John F.
                Kennedy as Secretary of Health, Education and Welfare.
                He had been Mayor of Cleveland from 1953 to 1962 and
                Senator in the Ohio State Legislature from 1952 to 1953.

1963   President John F. Kennedy, by special message to Con-
                gress, urged total revision of the anachronistic immigration
                legislation.   He asked for a law which would reflect "in
                every detail the principle of equality and human dignity,
                to which our Nation subscribes."

1963   Walter F. Alessandroni was appointed Attorney General of
                Pennsylvania by Governor William Scranton.

1963   John P. Lomenzo, presently the Secretary of State for
                New York State, was appointed by Governor Nelson D.
                Rockefeller.

1964   Pope Paul made his historic visit to the United Nations in
                New York City and spoke for world peace.

1964   John O. Pastore was the keynote speaker at the Democratic
                National Convention.

1964   The Verrazzano-Narrows Bridge was inaugurated on Nov-
                ember 21st. It is the longest single-span suspension
                bridge in the world.

1964   Teno Roncalio was elected United States Congressman
                representing the State of Wyoming and was re-elected
                in 1968.

1964   Luigi R. Marano was appointed Judge of the Family Court
                of the State of New York. As a member of the New York
                State Legislature (1956 to 1964) he co-sponsored a bill,
                passed into law, known as the PKU Bill, which mandates
                that new-born children be given a blood test to find pre-
                sence of the disease known as Phenolkenturia. Thousands
                of children were saved from mental retardation as a result.
                a result.

1964   Ralph J. Menconi, Sculptor, designed the John F. Kennedy
                Memorial Medal and the President Lyndon B. Johnson
                Medal. He produced more than 300 medallion portraits
                including those of fourteen Presidents.

1965   Joseph Anthony Califano, Jr. was appointed by President
                Lyndon B. Johnson as his Special Assistant.

1965   Following the strong pleas of four presidents - Truman,
                Eisenhower, Kennedy and Johnson - Congress passed the
                Immigration and Nationality Amendments of 1965. Said
                President Johnson, as he signed the bill into law, this
                "corrects a cruel and enduring wrong in the conduct of the
                American nation . . . . those who come will come because
                of what they are - not because of the land from which they
                spring." The amendments provide for the gradual elim-
                ination of the national origins formula   over a period of
                three years.

1965   Peter W. Rodino, United States Congressman from New
                Jersey, was instrumental in removing discriminatory
                national quotas and in humanizing the country's immigra-
                tion program by introducing a Bill to Amend the Immigra-
                tion and Nationality Act.

1965   Michael Musmanno, lawyer, judge and author, wrote The
                Italians in America. He was one of a team of lawyers de-
                fending Sacco and Vanzetti in the murder trial of 1927.

He wrote a strong plea in their defense in his book: After Twelve Years, 1939.   President Harry S. Truman appointed him one of the Presiding Judges at the International War Crimes Trials in Nuremberg in 1946.   He also authored his minority opinions while on the Pennsylvania bench, appropriately titled: Musmanno Dissents, 1939.   He is the author of numerous other writings; he held public office several times in his vibrant career.

1965   The Center for Migration Studies, Staten Island, New York, was formed to house and preserve documents, photographs, memoirs and private papers of organizations and individuals reflecting the experience of Italians in the United States.   The Center is open to researchers and graduate students interested in the history and sociology of the Italians in America.   Fathers Silvano and Lidio Tomasi, both of the Scalabrini Order, are in charge of the Center.

1966   Richard G. Ciccolella was promoted to Major General, October 19th.   He has had extensive experience on the battle fields of World War II, and Cambodia.   Also, in 1966, he served as Senior Member of the United Nations Command, Military Armistice Commission in the Republic of Korea at Panmunjom.   In 1970, he was assigned Chief of Staff of the First United States Army and is currently serving as Deputy Commanding General.

1966   Miss Jimilu Mason, noted sculptress of Alexandria, Virginia, whose mother is of Italian heritage, was commissioned to sculpt the official marble bust of President Lyndon B. Johnson to join those of other former Vice Presidents on display in the Senate wing of the Capitol and was appointed by the President to the National Council on the Arts.

1967   Peter W. Rodino, United States Congressman from New Jersey, succeeded in making Columbus Day a national holiday.   Recipient of numerous awards and decorations in recognition of his many contributions to a better America.

1967   Romano Mazzoli was the first Italian-American to be elected a United States Congressman representing the State of Kentucky.

1968   Francis J. Mugavero was ordained Bishop of the Diocese of Brooklyn, New York.   Bishop Mugavero was the first ecclesiastic of Italian extraction to achieve the highest office of one of the greatest dioceses in the world.

1968   Mario Biaggi was elected to the United States Congress and
               re-elected in 1970, for the 24th Congressional District,
               Bronx, New York.

1968   Joseph L. Alioto was elected Mayor of San Francisco, Cal-
               ifornia. The nominating speech for the 1968 Presiden-
               tial candidate, Hubert M. Humphrey, was delivered by him
               at the Democratic National Convention in Chicago, Illinois.

1968   Miss Jimilu Mason, sculpted the Brumidi bust of carrara
               marble in Pietrasanta, Italy. The bust is now in the
               "Brumidi corridor" on the first floor of the Senate wing
               of the Capitol.

1969   Salvador Luria, biologist, was the co-recipient of the Nobel
               Prize for Medicine; (discoveries concerning the replica-
               tion mechanism and the genetic structure of viruses).

1969   Edward Domenic Re was appointed Judge of the United
               States Customs Court. He served as Assistant Secretary
               of State for Educational and Cultural Affairs under Presi-
               dent Johnson, 1968 - 1969. Was Chairman of the Foreign
               Claims Settlement Commission of the United States from
               1961 to 1968. Was a member of the Board of Higher Edu-
               cation of the City of New York between 1954 and 1969. Was
               a law professor at St. John's University, School of Law,
               from 1947 to 1961 (thereafter on leave until 1969). Author
               of several leading law school texts: Foreign Confiscations
               in Anglo-American Law, 1951; Cases and Materials on
               International Law (with Lester B. Orfield), revised edi-
               tion 1965; Brief Writing and Oral Argument, 3rd edition,
               1965; Cases and Materials on Equity (with Zachariah
               Chafee, Jr.), 1967. Contributed numerous articles to
               periodicals.

1970   Sebastian (Sam) Leone was the first American of Italian
               extraction to serve as Borough President of Brooklyn,
               New York. This borough, because of its immense popu-
               lation, is often referred to as "the fourth largest city in
               America."

1970   M. Henry Martuscello was appointed by Governor Nelson
               A. Rockefeller as Associate Justice of the Appellate
               Division of the New York State Supreme Court. Prior
               to that, he was elected to the New York Supreme Court
               in 1952, re-elected in 1966. Co-author: New York
               Pattern Jury Instructions-Civil, 2 volumes.

CHARTER GRANTING CHRISTOPHER COLUMBUS
THE PREROGATIVES AND PRIVILEGES OF HIS VOYAGE - APRIL 30, 1492

For years Columbus went to the great sea-faring powers of his day - the Portuguese (most formidable of them all), the French, the English, finally the Spanish, to beg to be allowed to explore a new trade route to the fabulous lands of China and India. Columbus was worn out and impoverished in the attenpt. It was only through the good office of the Queen's own Chaplain, a monk, who befriended him in his need, that Columbus was able to secure the commitment of Ferdinand and Isabella, King and Queen of Castile. They outfitted a fleet of three vessels. The charter sets forth the conditions and the rewards of the venture.

Ferdinand and Elizabeth, . . .
For as much of you, Christopher Columbus, are going by our command, with some of our vessels and men, to discover and subdue some islands and Continent in the ocean, and it is hoped that by God's assistance, some of the said Islands and Continent in the ocean will be discovered and conquered by your means and conduct, therefore it is but just and reasonable, that since you expose yourself to such danger to serve us, you should be rewarded for it. And we being willing to honour and favour you for the reasons aforesaid; Our will is, That you, Christopher Columbus, after discovering and conquering the said Islands and Continent in the said ocean, or any of them, shall be our Admiral of the said Islands and Continent you shall so discover and conquer; and that you be our Admiral, Vice-Roy, and Governor in them, and that for the future, you may call and stile yourself, D. Christopher Columbus, and that your sons and successors in the said employment, may call themselves Dons, Admirals, Vice-Roys, and Governours of them; and that you may exercise the office of Admiral, with the charge of Vice-Roy and Governour of the said Islands and Continent, which you and your Lieutenants shall conquer and freely decide all causes, civil and criminal, appertaining to the said employment of Admiral, ViceRoy, and Governour, as you shall think fit in justice, and as the Admirals of our Kingdoms use to do; and that you have power to punish offenders; and you and your Lieutenants exercise the employments of Admiral, Vice-Roy, and Governour, in all things belonging to the said offices, or any of them; and that you enjoy the perquisites and salaries belonging to the said employments, and to each of them, in the same manner as the High Admiral of our kingdoms does. And by this our letter, or a copy of it signed by a Public Notary: We command Prince John, our most dearly beloved Son, the Infants, Dukes, Prelates, Marquesses, Great Masters and Military Orders, Priors, Commendaries, our Counsellors, Judges, and other Officers of Justice whatsoever, belonging to our Household, Courts, and Chancery, and Constables of Castles, Strong Houses, and others, and all Corporations, Bayliffs, Gov-

ernours, Judges, Commanders, Sea Officers; and the Aldermen, Common Council, Officers, and Good People of all Cities, Lands, and Places in our Kingdoms and Dominions, and in those you shall conquer and subdue, and the captains, masters, mates, and other officers and sailors, our natural subjects now being, or that shall be for the time to come, and any of them, that when you shall have discovered the said Islands and Continent in the ocean; and you, or any that shall have your commission, shall have taken the usual oath in such cases, that they for the future, look upon you as long as you live, and after you, your son and heir, and so from one heir to another forever, as our Admiral on our said Ocean, and as Vice-Roy and Governour of the said Islands and Continent, by you, Christopher Columbus, discovered and conquered; and that they treat you and your Lieutenants, by you appointed, for executing the employments of Admiral, Vice-Roy, and Governour, as such in all respects, and give you all the perquisites and other things belonging and appertaining to the said offices; and allow, and cause to be allowed you, all the honours, graces, concessions, prehaminences, prerogatives, immunities, and other things, or any of them which are due to you, by virtue of your commands of Admiral, Vice-Roy, and Governour, and to be observed completely, so that nothing be diminished; and that they make no objection to this, or any part of it, nor suffer it to be made; forasmuch as we from this time forward, by this our letter, bestow on you the employments of Admiral, Vice-Roy, and perpetual Governour forever; and we put you into possession of the said offices, and of every of them, and full power to use and exercise them, and to receive the perquisites and salaries belonging to them, or any of them, as was said above. Concerning all which things, if it be requisite, and you shall desire it, We command our Chancellour, Notaries, and other Officers, to pass, seal, and deliver to you, our Letter of Privilege, in such form and legal manner, as you shall require or stand in need of. And that none of them presume to do any thing to the contrary, upon pain of our displeasure, and fortfeiture of 30 ducats for each offence. And we command him, who shall show them this our Letter, that he summon them to appear before us at our Court, where we shall then be, within fifteen days after such summons, under the said penalty. Under which same, we also command any Public Notary whatsoever, that he give to him that shows it him, a certificate under his seal, that we may know how our command is obeyed.

Given at Granada, on the 30th of April, in the year of our Lord, 1492.

I, THE KING, I, THE QUEEN.

BOOK OF THE FIRST NAVIGATION AND DISCOVERY OF THE INDIES

> Columbus was a good navigator and as such he kept an accurate log or journal of his voyage into the unknown. The preamble, here set forth, is characteristic of the flowery expressions of his day. Nonetheless, it constitutes an entrancing sea journal, containing painstaking detail missing from the second-hand accounts with which we are all familiar.

In The Name Of Our Lord Jesus Christ

BECAUSE, most Christian and very exalted excellent and mighty Princes, King and Queen of the Spains and of the islands in the Sea, our Lord and Lady, in this present year 1492, after Your Highnesses had made an end to the war with the Moors who ruled in Europe, and had concluded the war in the very great city of Granada, where in the present year, on the second day of the month of January, by force of arms I saw the royal standards of Your Highnesses placed on the towers of Alhambra (which is the citadel of the said city), and I saw the Moorish King come forth to the gates of the city and kiss the royal hands of Your Highessses and of the Prince my lord, and soon after in that same month, through the information that I had given to Your Highnesses concerning the lands of India, and of a prince who is called "Grand Khan" which is to say in our vernacular "King of Kings," how many times he and his ancestors had sent to Rome to seek doctors in our Holy Faith to instruct him therein, and that never had the Holy Father provided them, and thus were lost so many people through lapsing into idolatries and receiving doctrines of perdition;

AND Your Highnesses, as Catholic Christians and Princes devoted to the Holy Christian Faith and the propagators thereof, and enemies of the sect of Mahomet and of all idolatries and heresies, resolved to send me Christopher Columbus to the said regions of India, to see the said princes and peoples and lands and [to observe] the disposition of them and of all, and the manner in which may be undertaken their conversion to our Holy Faith, and ordained that I should not go by land (the usual way) to the Orient, but by the route of the Occident, by which no one to this day knows for sure that anyone has gone;

THEREFORE, in the same month of January Your Highnesses commanded me that with a sufficient fleet I should go to the said regions of India, and for this granted me many rewards, and ennobled me so that henceforth I might call myself by a noble title and be Admiral-in-Chief of the Ocean Sea and Viceroy and Perpetual Governor of all the islands and mainlands that I should discover and win, or that henceforth might be discovered and won in the Ocean Sea, and that my eldest son should succeed me, and thus from rank to rank for ever.

AND I departed from the city of Granada on the 12th day of the month of May of the same year 1492, on a Saturday, and came to the town of Palos, which is a seaport, where I fitted for sea three ships well suited for such an undertaking, and I departed from the said harbor well furnished with much provision and many seamen, on the third day of the month of August of the said year, on a Friday, at half an hour before sunrise, and took the route for the Canary Islands of Your Highnesses, which are in the said Ocean, that I might thence take my course and sail until I should reach the Indies, and give the letters of Your Highnesses to those princes, and thus comply with what you had commanded.

AND for this I thought to write down upon this voyage in great detail from day to day all that I should do and see, and encounter, as hereinafter shall be seen.   In addition, Lord Princes, to noting down each night what that day had brought forth, and each day what was sailed by night, I have the intention to make a new chart of navigation, upon which I shall place the whole sea and lands of the Ocean Sea in their proper positions under their bearings, and further to compose a book, and set down everything as in a real picture, by latitude north of the equator and longitude west; and above all it is very important that I forget sleep and labor much at navigation because it is necessary.   All of which will be great labor.

COLUMBUS' REPORT TO THE KING & QUEEN OF SPAIN

> The Letter of Columbus reporting his discoveries to King
> Ferdinand and Queen Isabella of Spain. (Note that Columbus
> is convinced he had reached "the continental province of
> Cathay.")

A Letter addressed to the noble Lord Raphael Sanchez, Treasurer
to their most invincible Majesties, Ferdinand and Isabella, King
and Queen of Spain, by Christopher Columbus, to whom our age is
greatly indebted, treating of the islands of India recently discovered
beyond the Ganges, to explore which he had been sent eight months
before under the auspices and at the expense of their said Majesties.

Knowing that it will afford you pleasure to learn that I have brought
my undertaking to a successful termination, I have decided upon writing
you this letter to acquaint you with all the events which have occurred in
my voyage, and the discoveries which have resulted from it.   Thirty-three
days after my departure from Cadiz' I reached the Indian sea, where I
discovered many islands, thickly peopled, of which I took possession without resistance in the name of our most illustrious Monarch, by public pro-
clamation and with unfurled banners.   To the first of these islands, which
is called by the Indians Guanahani, I gave the name of the blessed Saviour
(San Salvador), relying upon whose protection I had reached this as well
as the other islands; to each of these I also gave a name, ordering that one
should be called Santa Maria de la Concepcion, another Fernandina, the third
Isabella, the fourth Juana, and so with all the rest respectively.   As soon
as we arrived at that, which as I have said was named Juana, I proceeded
along its coast a short distance westward, and found it to so large and
apparently without termination, that I could not suppose it to be an island,
but the continental province of Cathay.   Seeing, however, no towns or pop-
ulous places on the sea coast, but only a few detached houses and cottages,
with whose inhabitants I was unable to communicate, because they fled
as soon as they saw us, I went further on, thinking that in my progress I
should certainly find some city or village.   At length, after proceeding a
great way and finding that nothing new presented itself, and that the line of
coast was leading us northwards (which I wished to avoid, because it was
winter, and it was my intention to move southwards; and because moreover
the winds were contrary), I resolved not to attempt any further progress, but
rather to turn back and retrace my course to a certain bay that I had observed, and from which I afterwards dispatched two of our men to ascertain
whether there were a king or any cities in that province.   These men re-
connoitred the country for three days, and found a most numerous population, and great numbers of houses, though small, and built without any regard to order: with which information they returned to us.   In the mean-
time I had learned from some Indians whom I had seized, that that country was certainly an island: and therefore I sailed towards the east, coast-

ing to the distance of three hundred and twenty-two miles, which brought
us to the extremity of it; from this point I saw lying eastwards another island, fifty-four miles distant from Juana, to which I gave the name of Es-
panola.

LETTERS PATENT TO JOHN CABOT
March 5, 1496

>   John Cabot, a Genoese, had settled among the adventurous
>   merchants of Bristol, England. He persuaded King Henry VII
>   to sponsor a new attempt to find a northern route to the rich
>   markets of the East.   This document formalized the agreement.

The Letters patents of King Henry the seuenth granted unto John
Cabot and his three sonnes, Lewis, Sebastian, and Sancius for the discouerie
of new and unknowen lands.

HEnry, by the grace of God, king of England and France, and lord of
Ireland, to all to whom these presents shall come, Greeting.

Be it knowen that we haue giuen and granted, and by these presents
do giue and grant for vs and our heires, to our welbeloued John Cabot
citizen of Venice, to Lewis, Sebastian, and Santius, sonnes of the sayd John,
and to the heires of them, and euery of them, and their deputies, full and
free authority, leaue, and power to saile to all parts, countreys, and seas
of the East, of the West, and of the North, under our banners and ensignes,
with fiue ships of what burthen or quantity soeuer they be, and as many
mariners or men as they will haue with them in the sayd ships, upon their
owne proper costs and charges, to seeke out, discouer, and finde whatsoeuer
isles, countreys, regions or prouinces of the heathen and infidels whatsoeuer they be, and in what part of the world soeuer they be, which before
this time haue bene unknowen to all Christians: we haue granted to them,
and also to euery of them, the heires of them, and euery of them, and their
deputies, and haue giuen them licence to set vp our banners and ensignes
in euery village, towne, castle, isle, or maine land of them newly found.
And that the aforesayd Iohn and his sonnes, or their heires and assignes
may subdue, occupy and possesse all such townes, cities, castles and isles
of them found, which they can subdue, occupy and possesse, as our vassals,
and lieutenants, getting into vs the rule, title, and iurisdiction of the same
villages, townes, castles & firme land so found.   Yet so that the aforesayd
Iohn, and his sonnes and heires, and their deputies, be holden and bounden
of all the fruits, profits, gaines, and commodities growing of such nauigation, for euery their voyage, as often as they shall arriue at our port of
Bristoll (at which port they shall be bound and holden onely to arriue) all
manner of necessary costs and charges by them made, being deducted, to
pay into us in wares or money the fift part of the capitall gaine so gotten.
We giuing and granting into them and to their heires and deputies, that they
shall be free from all paying of customes of all and singular such merchan-
dize as they shall be free from all paying of customes of all and singular
they shall bring with them from those places so newlie found.

And moreouer, we haue given and granted to them, their heires and
deputies, that all the firme lands, isles, villages, townes, castles and places
whatsoeuer they be that they shall chance to finde, may not of any other of
our subjects be frequented or visited without the licence of the foresayd
Iohn and his sonnes, and their deputies, under payne of forfeiture as well
of their ships as of all and singular goods of all them that shall presume

33

to saile to those places so found.   Willing, and most straightly commanding all and singular our subjects as well on land as on sea, appointed officers, to giue good assistance to the aforesaid Iohn, and his sonnes and deputies, and that as well in arming and furnishing their ships or vessels, as in prouision of quietnesse, and in buying of victuals for their money, and all other things by them to be prouided necessary for the sayd nauigation, they do giue them all their helpe and fauour.   In witnesse whereof we have caused to be made these our lettres patents.   Witnesse our selfe at West-minister, the fift day of March, in the eleuenth yeere of our reigne.----

Amerigo Vespucci, by some strange circumstance, had his name affixed to the New World. This on the strength of his vivid, first-hand observations and recordings made during his voyages to the Americas. The excerpt below is taken from his famous letter to Soderini which constitutes his report of his voyages.

My Magnificent Lord, Your Magnificence doubtless knows [that] the reason of my coming to this realm of Spain was to engage in commerce, and that I persisted in this purpose about four years, during which I saw and experienced the varied turns of Fortune, and how she kept changing these frail and fleeting benefits, and how at one time she holds man at the top of her wheel, and again hurls him from her, and deprives him of that wealth which may be called borrowed. So when I had come to know the constant toil which man exerts in gaining it, by subjecting himself to so many discomforts and perils, I resolved to abandon trade, and to aspire to something more praiseworthy and enduring. So it came about that I arranged to go to see a portion of the world and its marvels. Time and place greatly favored me in this, for it happened that King Don Ferdinand of Castile, having occasion to send four ships westward to discover new lands, I was chosen by His Highness to go in this fleet to aid in the discovery. And we set forth from the port of Cadiz, the 10th of May, 1497, and set our course over the great expanse of the Ocean Sea, in which voyage we spent 18 months; and we discovered much continental land and islands without number, and a great share of them inhabited, of which no mention is made by the ancient (fol. 2v, M) writers; because they had no knowledge [of them,] I believe. For, if I remember rightly, I have read in some one of these that he held that the Ocean Sea was devoid of inhabitants; and of this opinion was Dante, our poet, in the 26th chapter of the Inferno, where he invents the death of Ulysses. On this voyage I saw things of great wonder, as Your Magnificence will hear.

As I said above, we departed from the port of Cadiz, four consort ships, (fol. 2v, P) and began our cruise straight for the Isles of the Blest, which are to-day called the Grand Canary, which are situated in the Ocean Sea at the end of the inhabited west, set in the third climate, above which the north pole has an elevation of 27 2/3 degrees over their horizon; and they are 280 leagues distant from this city of Lisbon, [in which this present work is written,] on the course between south and south-west.

[There] we lingered eight days, providing ourselves with water and wood and other necessary things. And from here, having said our prayers, we started and set sail, beginning our voyage toward the west, taking one quarter by southwest. And we sailed until after 37 days we reached a land which we judged to be continental, which is distant westward from the Canary Isles about one thousand leagues beyond the inhabited region, within the torrid zone; because we found the north pole elevated 16 degrees above its horizon, and westward of the Canary Isles, as our instruments showed. (fol. 3r, M) 75 degrees. Here we anchored our ships a league and a half off land; and we cast off our boats laden with men and arms. We proceeded toward land, and before we reached it, sighted many people who were walking along the shore, whereat we greatly rejoiced. And we found them to be a naked race. They showed fear of us, I think because they saw us [clothed] and of an appearance different [from theirs.] All withdrew to a mountain, and, in spite of all the signs of peace and friendship we made to them, they would not come to converse with us. So, inasmuch as night was already falling, and because the ships were anchored in a perilous place, being on a forbidding coast and without shelter, we resolved to betake ourselves thence on the morrow and to go in quest of some port or bay where we might place our ships in safety. And we sailed north-west, for thus the coast trended, ever in sight of land, continually seeing people along the beach, until, after having voyaged two days, we found a tolerably safe place for the ships. And we anchored a half league from shore, where we saw an immense number of people. And this same day we went ashore with the boats. And we leaped ashore, full 40 well equipped men, and the people ashore still showed themselves shy of associating with us. And we could not so reassure them that they would come to talk with us. And this day we so persistently endeavored in giving them of our wares, such as bells, mirrors, glass beads and other (fol. 3v, M) trash that some of them were rendered confident, and came (fol. 3r. P) to converse with us. And when we had established kindly relations with them, inasmuch as night was falling, we took leave of them and returned to the ships. And the next day, when dawn broke, we saw that infinite hordes were on the beach; and they had with them their wives and children. We put ashore and found that all came laden with their possessions, which are such as will be told in its place. And before we reached land, many of them dove and came [to meet] us a cross-bow shot out to sea, for they are very great swimmers, with just as much confidence as if they had associated with us for a long time. And we were pleased at this confidence of theirs. [Inasmuch as the opportunity offers, we weave into our narrative, here and in other places, those of their customs which we saw them possessed of.]

In 1519, Ferdinand Magellan set out on his historic voyage to the Moluccas (an island group of what is now Indonesia - also called the Spice Islands). Actually, it turned out to be a trip around the world - the first. Magellan never lived to see the end of it, but a faithful recorder, Pigafetta, by name, kept a painstaking, detailed account running well over a hundred pages. The introductory paragraphs follow.

Forasmuch as (most illustrious and very reverend Lord) there are divers curious persons who not only take pleasure in hearing and knowing the great and marvelous things which God has permitted me to see and suffer during the long and perilous voyage which I have made, hereafter written, but who also wish to know the means and fashion and the road which I took to go thither, not lending faith or firm belief to the end until they are first informed and assured of the beginning: wherefore, my Lord, be pleased to understand that, finding myself in Spain, in the year of the Nativity of our Lord 1519, at the court of the most serene King of the Romans, with the reverend Monsignor, master Francesco Chieregati, then apostolic protonotary and ambassador of Pope Leo X (and who has since by his virtue attained to the bishopric of Aprutino and principality of Teramo), and having learned, both by reading of divers books and from the report of many clerks and learned men who discussed the great and terrible things of the Ocean Sea with the said protonotary, I determined (by the good favor of the Emperor and the above-mentioned lord) to experience and to go to see some of the said things, thereby $f3^v$ to satisfy the wishes of the said lords and also mine, that it might be told that I made the voyage and saw with my eyes the things hereafter written, and that I might win a famous name with posterity.

Now, to come to unfold the beginning of my voyage (most illustrious lord), having heard that there was in the city of Seville a small fleet to the number of five ships ready to make that long voyage, that is, to find and discover the isles of Molucca whence come the spices (of which fleet the captain-general was Fernao de Magalhaes, a Portuguese gentleman, commander of the Order of Santiago de la Spada, who had made several voyages in the Ocean Sea in which he had deported himself honorably and as a man of worth), I set out with several letters of recommendation from Barcelona, where at that time the Emperor was, and came by sea to Malaga. And from the sea I went by land until I reached the above-mentioned city of Seville, where I abode the space of three months waiting for the said fleet to be put in order and prepared for its voyage.

And inasmuch (most illustrious lord) as on my return from the voyage, going to Rome to visit our Holy Father, I found your lordship at Monterosi where of your grace you made me welcome and later gave me to understand that you desired to have in writing the things which God by his grace allowed me to see in my said voyage: therefore to satisfy and yield to your wish I have set down in this little book the principal things as best I could.

Finally (most illustrious lord), all preparations having been made and the ships put in order, the captain-general, a wise and virtuous man and mindful of his honor, would not begin his voyage without first issuing some good and honorable regulations, as it is the good custom to make for those who go to sea. But he did not wholly declare the voyage which he wished to make, lest the people from astonishment and fear refuse to accompany him on so long a voyage as he had in mind to undertake, in view of the great and violent storms of the Ocean Sea whither he would go. And for another reason also.

For the masters and captains of the other ships of his company loved him not. I do not know the reason, unless it be that he, the captain-general, was Portuguese, and they were Spaniards or Castilians, which peoples have long borne ill-will and malevolence toward one another. Notwithstanding, they all held obedience to him and he made his regulations as follows, that in the hazards of the sea (which often occur by night and by day) the ships should not go astray and separate from each other. Which regulations he published and issued in writing to each ship's master, and ordered that they be observed and kept inviolably, unless with great and legitimate excuse and evidence of being unable to do otherwise.

On Saturday the sixth of September, one thousand five hundred and twenty-two, we entered the Bay of San Lucar, and we were only eighteen men, the most part sick, of the sixty remaining who had left Molucca, some of whom died of hunger, others deserted at the island of Timor, and others had been put to death for their crimes.

From the time when we departed from that Bay until the present day we had sailed fourteen thousand four hundred and sixty leagues, and completed the circuit of the world from east to west.

On Monday the eighth of September we cast anchor near the Mole of Seville, and there we discharged all the artillery. And on Tuesday we all went, in our shirts and barefoot, and each with a torch in his hand, to visit the shrine of Santa Maria de la Victoria and that of Santa Maria de Antigua.

Departing from Seville, I went to Valladolid, where I presented to his Sacred Majesty Don Carlos, not gold or silver, but something to be prized by such a lord. And among other things I gave him a book written by my hand treating of all the things that had occurred day by day on our voyage. Then I departed thence, and went to Portugal, where I spoke with the King, Dom Joao, of the things which I had seen. And, passing through Spain, I came into France where I made a gift of some things from the other hemisphere to Madame the Regent, mother of the very Christian King Francois. Then I came into Italy, where I established my abode forever, and I devoted my vacations and vigils to the most illustrious and noble lord, Philippe de Villiers L'Isle-Adam, the very worthy Grand Master of Rhodes.

END

PHILIP MAZZEI ON THE NATURAL RIGHTS OF MAN

The fabulous Philip Mazzei was a close friend of Jefferson. They were kindred spirits, aroused by the tyranny of England and stimulated by the vision of freedom for all men. This extract from Mazzei's article in the Virginia Gazette under the pseudonym "Furioso" appeared sometime in 1774-1775. (Note the similarity of language in the American Declaration of Independence, July 4, 1776.)

To attain our goal it is necessary, my dear fellow-citizens, to discuss the natural rights of man and the foundations of a free government . . . . All men are by nature equally free and independent. This equality is essential to the establishment of a liberal government. Every individual must be equal to every other in his natural rights. The division of society into ranks has always been and will always continue to be a serious obstacle to the attainment of this end . . . . I repeat that a truly republican form of government cannot exist except where all men --- from the very rich to the very poor --- are perfectly equal in their natural rights. Fortunately, we are now free on this continent . . . . Now when certain privileges are exercised by a portion of the inhabitants and denied to others, it is vain to hope for the establishment of a liberal and permanent government, unless the favored citizens are willing to relinquish their privileges and stand on a footing of perfect equality with the rest of the inhabitants. Discrimination inevitably arouses envy and ill-feeling . . . . Therefore, liberty will always be insecure and finally doomed to collapse . . . . Democracy, I mean representative democracy, which embraces all individuals in one simple body, without any distinction whatsoever, is certainly the only form of government under which a true and enduring liberty may be enjoyed. Unfortunately for mankind, this form of government has never existed. The sacred name of democracy has been abused by tumultuous governments built on false and unstable principles . . . .

BENJAMIN FRANKLIN'S LETTER TO MAZZEI

Benjamin Franklin was also a friend of the progressive Philip Mazzei. He wrote him a welcome letter in 1775 commenting on Mazzei's introduction of new horticultural products. The Walpole incident, referred to in the document, had to do with some difficulty about Chinese textiles.

Philadelphia, dicember 27, 1775.

Dear Sir,

It was with great pleasure I learnt from Mr. Jefferson, that you were settled in America, and from the letter you favoured me with, that you like the Country, and have reason to expect success in your laudable and meritorious endeavours to introduce new products. I heartly wish you all the success you can desire in that and in every other undertaking that may conduce to your comfortable establishment in your present situation.

I know not how it has happened, that you did not receive an answer to your letter from the secretaries of our Society. I suppose they must have written, and that it has miscarried.---If you have not yet sent the Books, which the Academy of Turin have done us the honour to present us with, we must, I fear, wait for more quiet Times before we can have the pleasure of receiving them, the communication being now very difficult.

I can hardly suspect Mr. Walpole of the Practise against you, which you mention, especially as he was then expecting to have lands of his own in America, wherein the productions you were about to introduce must have been beneficial. I rather suspect a person whom you may remember was frequently with him; I meam [sic] Martinelli. I rejoice that you escaped the snares that were laid for you, and I think all America is obliged to the Great Duke for his benevolence towards it, in the protection he afforded you, and his encouragement of your undertaking.

We have experienced that silk may be produced to great advantage. While in London i [sic] had some trunks full sent me from hence three years successively, and it sold by auction for about 19/6 the small pound, which was not much below the silk from Italy.

The Congress have not yet extended their vieux [sic] much towards foreign Powers. They are nevertheless obliged by your kind offers of your service, which perhaps in a year or two more may become very useful to them. I am myself much pleased, that you have sent a Translation of our Declaration to the Grand Duke; because having a high esteem of the Character of that Prince, and of the whole Imperial Family, from the accounts given me of them by my friend Dr. Ingenhousz and yourself, I should be happy to find that we stood well in the opinion of that Court.

Mr. Fromond of Milan, with whom I had the pleasure of being acquainted in London, spoke to me of a plant much used in Italy, and which he thought would be useful to us in America. He promised at my request to send me some of the seeds, which he has accordingly done. I have unfortunately forgotten the uses, and Know nothing of the culture. In both these particulars I must beg information and advise from you. It is called Ravizzoni.

I send specimens of the seed inclosed.

    I received from the same Mr. Fromond four copies of a translation of some of my Pieces into the fine language of your native Country. I beg your acceptance of one of them, and of my best wishes for your whealth [sic] and prosperity.

    With great esteem and regard, I have the honor to be,

    Dear Sir

        Your most obedient and most humble Servant

                              B. Franklin.

BOTTA'S HISTORY OF THE REVOLUTIONARY WAR

Charles Botta, in 1839, wrote the first extensive history of the struggle of the Thirteen Colonies for independence from England. He entitled it a History of the War of the Independence of the United States of America. Botta's account of Washington's farewell address is a touching scene.

The army was disbanded; but the supreme command still remained in the hands of Washington: the public mind was intent upon what he was about to do. His prudence reminded him that it was time to put a term to the desire of military glory; his thoughts were now turned exclusively upon leaving to his country a great example of moderation. The congress was then in session at the city of Annapolis in Maryland. Washington communicated to that body his resolution to resign the command, and requested to know whether it would be their pleasure that he should offer his resignation in writing, or at an audience. The congress answered, that they appointed the twenty-third of December for that ceremony. When this day arrived, the hall of congress was crowded with spectators; the legislative and executive characters of the state, several general officers, and the consul-general of France, were present. The members of congress remained seated and covered. The spectators were standing and uncovered. The general was introduced by the secretary, and conducted to a seat near the president. After a decent interval, silence was commanded, and a short pause ensued. The president, general Mifflin, then informed him, that the United States in congress assembled were prepared to receive his communications. Washington rose, and with an air of inexpressible dignity, delivered the following address:---

'Mr. President; The great events on which my resignation depended having at length taken place, I have now the honor of offering my sincere congratulations to congress, and of presenting myself before them to surrender into their hands the trust committed to me and to claim the indulgence of retiring from the service of my country. Happy in the confirmation of our independence and sovereignty, and pleased with the opportunity afforded the United States of becoming a respectable nation, I resign with satisfaction the appointment I accepted with diffidence, a diffidence in my abilities to accomplish so arduous a task, which, however, was superseded by a confidence in the rectitude of our cause, the support of the supreme power of the Union, and the patronage of Heaven. The successful termination of the war has verified the most sanguine expectations; and my gratitude for the interposition of Providence, and the assistance I have received from my countrymen, increases with every review of the momentous contest. While I repeat my obligations to the army in general, I should do injustice to my own feelings not to acknowledge, in this place, the peculiar services and distinguished merits of the gentlemen who have been attached to my person during the war. It was impossible the choice of confidential officers to compose my family should have been more fortunate. Permit me, sir, to recommend, in particular, those who have continued in the service to the present moment, as worthy of the favorable notice and patronage of congress.

'I consider it as an indispensable duty to close this last act of my official life by commending the interests of our dearest country to the protection of Almighty God, and those who have the superintendence of them to his holy keeping. Having now finished the work assigned me, I retire from the great theater of action, and bidding an affectionate farewell to this august body, under whose orders I have so long acted, I here offer my commission, and take my leave of all the employments of public life.'

Having spoken thus, he advanced to the chair of the president, and deposited the commission in his hands. The president made him, in the name of congress, the following answer:---

'Sir; The United States, in congress assembled, receive with emotions too affecting for utterance, the solemn resignation of the authorities under which you have led their troops with success through a perilous and a doubtful war. Called upon by your country to defend its invaded rights, you accepted the sacred charge, before it had formed alliances, and while it was without funds or a government to support you. You have conducted the great military contest with wisdom and fortitude, invariably regarding the rights of the civil power, through all disasters and changes. You have, by the love and confidence of your fellow-citizens, enabled them to display their martial genius, and transmit their fame to posterity. You have persevered, until the United States, aided by a magnanimous king and nation, have been enabled, under a just Providence, to close the war in freedom, safety, and independence; on which happy event, we sincerely join you in congratulations. Having defended the standard of liberty in this new world, having taught a lesson useful to those who inflict, and to those who feel oppression, you retire from the great theater of action, with the blessing of your fellow-citizens; but the glory of your virtues will not terminate with your military command; it will continue to animate the remotest ages. We feel, with you, our obligations to the army in general, and will particularly charge ourselves with the interests of those confidential officers who have attended your person to this affecting moment. We join you in commending the interests of our dearest country to the protection of Almighty God, beseeching him to dispose the hearts and minds of its citizens to improve the opportunity afforded them of becoming a happy and respectable nation. And for you, we address to Him our earnest prayers that a life so beloved may be fostered with all his care; that your days may be happy as they have been illustrious; and that he will finally give you that reward which this world cannot give.'

When the president had terminated his discourse, a long and profound silence pervaded the whole assembly. All minds appeared impressed with the grandeur of the scene, the recollections of the past, the felicity of the present, and the hopes of the future. The captain-general and congress were the objects of universal eulogium.

A short time after this ceremony, Washington retired to enjoy the long desired repose of his seat of Mount Vernon, in Virginia.

THE GARIBALDI AND MEUCCI MEMORIAL MUSEUM
Rosebank, Staten Island, New York

In this house GIUSEPPE GARIBALDI took refuge after the fall of the Roman Republic in 1849 which he and Mazzini had defended to the bitter end against the overwhelming forces of Napoleon III. Between 1850 and 1854, with a long interval at sea to Asia and South America, Garibaldi lived here, a guest of Antonio Meucci (whose work was decisive in creating the telephone). Staten Island, at the time, was a small rural community. For a living, Garibaldi hunted, fished and made candles for sale by dipping wick into wax in the cauldron at the rear of the house. Already a legendary world figure for his leadership in the wars to free South America, he still had before him his greatest feat: the leading of the "One Thousand" to Sicily in 1860 to defeat the armies of the Bourbon Kings, liberate the South and achieve the unification of Italy. Here, on Staten Island, in the protective shadow of the Stars and Stripes, the man later to be known as the "Hero of Two Worlds" and the greatest fighter for democracy of the 19th Century nursed his wounds between wars dreaming of a day in which not his alone, but all peoples would be free.

44

GARIBALDI'S LETTER TO DANA (TRANSLATION)

The letter of Giuseppe Garibaldi, the Italian patriot, who sought political refuge in America after his defeat against the French. Mr. Charles Anderson Dana, the addressee, was the militant editor of the New York Tribune and (Princess) Belgioioso (of whom he writes) was leader of a volunteer committee for the help of the wounded at the siege of Rome in 1849. (The original is in Italian, translation by the editor.)

New York 27 April 1851

Mr. Dana,

I am very sorry I could not keep my appointment with you yesterday; and I wish I could excuse myself personally. I shall make every effort to satisfy my wish and avail myself of the honor of knowing you. However, since I'll be leaving this city for a long trip, I ask that you communicate with me the burden of the Belgioioso matter in writing, care of the Delmonico Hotel, before 2:00 p.m. tomorrow (April 28). At any rate please allow me the privilege of your friendship and let me be your faithful servant.

G. Garibaldi

MARCONI'S LETTER ON WIRELESS TELEGRAPHY

In response to the inquiry of many Americans, Guglielmo Marconi, the inventor of wireless telegraphy, wrote the following description of his invention for the readers of the <u>North American Review.</u>

The subject of Wireless Telegraphy has apparently caused some little interest among my friends, and among the inhabitants generally of the vast continent of America; and it is with no small amount of pleasure that I comply with the request to write a few words relative to the experiments and installations which have been carried out under my supervision.

I shall endeavour, in as brief a space as possible, to place a few facts before my readers to enable them to grasp the means by which these experiments have been brought to such a practical and successful issue.

My first experiments were conducted in 1895, on my father's estate in Bologna in Italy, and I was much surprised at the facility with which I found it possible to transmit messages without a wire for many miles.

On coming to England on private business in 1896, I was advised by my friends and relations to give a demonstration of the capabilities of my invention to the British Authorities who gave me facilities to test the system, and we were soon doing 9 miles across the Bristol Channel.

But, perhaps, at this point, it will not be out of place to give a brief description of the apparatus avoiding technicalities as much as possible.

We will first take the transmitting or sending apparatus.

I use an ordinary 10" Induction Coil, somewhat similar to the familiar shocking coil, but on a much larger scale.

Connected to the terminals of the Secondary winding, are two small spheres, about one or two centimeters apart.

Between these spheres the spark passes, and sets up the oscillations necessary for the transmission of signals.

When long distances are to be bridged, a vertical insulated conductor, suspended by means of a mast, is attached to one sphere, and the other sphere is connected to Earth.

If an ordinary telegraphic Key connecting a battery with the Coil be pressed, the Current from the battery is allowed to actuate the Spark Coil which charges the Vertical Conductor, and discharges across the gap separating the two spheres.

This discharge is an oscillating one, and the Insulated Conductor becomes a powerful radiator of Electric waves.

It will be easy to see how, by pressing the Key for long or short intervals, it is possible to Emit a long or short succession of Waves, which, when they influence the receiver, reproduce on it a long or short effect according to their duration, in this way reproducing Morse signals.

The principal point in my receiver is the Sensitive Tube or Radio Conductor, or, as it is generally termed, the Coherer.

It consists of a small glass tube, about four Centimeters in length, into which two Silver plugs are tightly filled.

A small gap separates them, and in this gap a mixture of Nickel and Silver filings are placed.

Under ordinary conditions, the resistance of this gap is too high to allow of any current passing from the local cell or battery; but, under the influence of Electric Waves, these filings instantly Cohere, and the tube becomes a comparatively good conductor.

Connected to this tube is a cell and a relay.

By the Cohesion of the filings, the current from the Cell is allowed to pass through the tube and actuate the relay.

When once this is achieved, it becomes a very simple matter to make a bell ring or to work an ordinary Morse Inkwriter.

But one peculiarity with this Cohesion of the filings, under the influence of an Electric wave, is their power of remaining cohered unless tapped or shaken up.

I have overcome this difficulty by using an automatic tapper or de-coherer, which is somewhat similar to an Electric bell tapper minus the bell.

This is so adjusted as to tap the tube and shake the filings up, thus decohering them and bringing them to their normal condition, when they are again in a state to receive another impulse.

This is worked by the relay and another local battery.

It will now be easy to follow the various actions which take place, namely, the oscillations set up by the transmitter at the distant station on the vertical conductor or resonator which is connected to the sensitive tube at the receiving station, cohere the filings in this tube, and allow the local cell to actuate the relay.

The relay, in its turn, causes the larger battery to pass a current through the tapper or interrupter, and also through the Electro magnets of the recording Instrument.

The practical result is that the Receiver is actuated for a time equal to that during which the key is pressed at the transmitting station.

With apparatus as thus explained and with the addition of a few important details which for brevity I shall not describe, I have made most of my experiments and worked numerous important installations.

After the experiments across the Bristol Channel, previously mentioned, I gave some important demonstrations to the Italian Naval Authorities at Spezia.

With the transmitter on shore and the Receiver on board an Italian Warship, a distance of twelve miles was bridged.

A series of trials were also carried out with other ships, and between ship and ship, and the Italian Navy were not slow in permanently adopting my system.

On Salisbury Plain I introduced Kites as a meaning of raising and suspending the vertical conductor to a considerable altitude.

It was during these Experiments that I attained my greatest distances between Salisbury and Bath, a distance of 34 miles.

Immediately after this, I set up two Experimental Stations, one at Alum Bay in the Isle of Wight, and the other at Bournemouth, the distance between them being fourteen miles, in order to test the practicability of the System under all conditions of Weather, and also to afford an opportunit of proving that "Wireless Telegraphy" was not a myth but a working reality.

It has, apparently, been thought that the weather, or varying Conditions of Atmospheric Electricity, may interfere with or stop the Signals transmitted by this system; but experience of over fourteen months of continual Everyday work has brought me to the conclusion, that there is no weather which can stop or seriously interfere with the working of such an installation.

We have given demonstrations to several eminent scientists who came down, often when we did not expect them; but on no occasion have they found any difficulty in the work of transmitting or receiving messages between the two stations.

Among others who inspected these stations, was Lord Kelvin, and he was kind enough to express himself as being highly pleased with what he saw.

He sent several telegrams to his friends and insisted on paying one shilling royalty on each message, wishing in this way to show his appreciation of what was done, and to illustrate its fitness at that time for Commercial purposes.

In July of last year, we gave an interresting demonstration at Kingstown Regatta, in reporting from a tug the results and incidents of the several yacht races. The relative positions of the Various Yachts were thus Wirelessly signalled, while the races were in progress, sometimes over a distance of ten miles, and published long before the yachts had returned to harbour. On one of these Excursions, we had the Company of several Stockbrokers and business men of Dublin, who transacted business on the receipt of the daily Stock Exchange quotations being sent off from our shore station, much to the amusement of all on board.

After finishing at Kingstown, I had the honour of being asked to instal wireless telegraphic Communication between the Royal Yacht, "Osborne" and Osborne House in the Isle of Wight, in order that Her Majesty might communicate with H. R. H. the Prince of Wales, who at the time was suffering from a fractured Knee. Altho quite hidden from one another by intervening hills and trees, constant and uninterrupted communication was maintained. This circumstance would have rendered direct signalling between the two positions impossible by means of any flag, semaphore or heliograph system. About 200 messages were sent, being chiefly private communications between the Queen and the Prince.

In December of last year, it was thought desirable to demonstrate that the system was quite practical and available for enabling telegraphic communication to be established between lightships and the shore. This as you are aware is a matter of great importance. By the Kind permission of the officials of Trinity House, we connected the East Goodwin Lightship - the outermost Lightship guarding the dangerous Goodwin Sands - with the South Foreland Lighthouse, a distance of twelve miles separating them. The apparatus was taken on board in an open boat and rigged up in one afternoon.

The installation started working from the very first without the slightest difficulty and it has continued to work admirably thro' all the storms which during this year have been so severe. By its means two vessels have already received quick and valuable assistance. Both ran on the sands in a fog. The Lightship noted their signals of distress, telegraphed for assistance, indicating the Exact spot where it was required, and tugs and lifeboats were soon rendering every aid. Various members of the Crew have learned how to send and receive signals and in fact run the station. Previous to our visit to the ship it is highly probable they had scarcely heard of Wireless Telegraphy, and were certainly unacquainted with even the rudiments of Electricity. This Knowledge is very valuable when the assistant, who is a poor Sailor, is unable to attend to it himself.

The latest installation that I have fitted up is across the English Channel, between the South Foreland Lighthouse and Boulogne, a distance of about thirty miles. This has worked with great success from the start, and at the present moment a message is being received respecting a vessel which has run on shore close to Wimereux.

The French authorities are most enthusiastic over the results.

All the above experiments have been made with what we term the Vertical Wire System; but I think it would be desirable, before closing this summary of events, to bring before my readers some observations on the use of parabolic reflectors, as a means of controling the propagation and intensifying the effects of these waves.

As in ordinary optics, so also in the optics of Electro magnetic oscillations, it is possible to reflect the waves radiated from the oscillator in one definite direction only.

The advantages obtainable by their use are obvious.

With the Vertical Wire System, the waves have been allowed to radiate in all directions and would affect all suitable receivers within a certain radius, altho it is possible by means of syntonising arrangements to prevent this to a certain Extent.

By means of reflectors it is possible to project the waves in one almost parallel beam, which will not affect any receiver placed out of its line of propagation.

This would Enable several forts or Islands to Communicate with Each other without any fear of the Enemy's tapping or interfering with the signals; for if the forts are situated on small heights, the beam of rays would pass above the position which might be held by an enemy.

The possibilities and importance of the uses to which these reflected radiations can be adapted are enormous.

More especially will this system be applicable to Enable ships to be warned by Lighthouses, Lightships or other Vessels, not only of their proximity to danger, but also of the direction from which the warning comes.

From the above brief and somewhat incomplete summary of what has actually been accomplished, and of what is being done every day, I trust the readers of the <u>North American Review</u> will be in a better state than hitherto, to form an opinion of the merits and possibilities of Wireless Telegraphy.

G. Marconi

South Foreland Lighthouse
Dover

1889

MARCONIGRAMS

Guglielmo Marconi, travelling on the Lucania of the Cunard Line to the United States in 1902, issued during the trip daily news items transmitted to the ship by wireless telegraphy. The news items appeared as the Cunard Daily Bulletin, the first of its kind on a pleasure, transoceanic vessel.

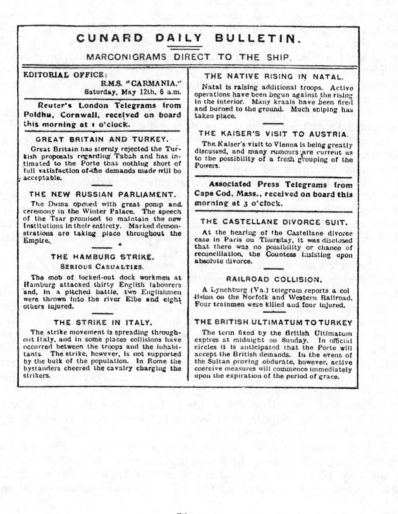

CUNARD DAILY BULLETIN.

MARCONIGRAMS DIRECT TO THE SHIP.

EDITORIAL OFFICE:
R.M.S. "CARMANIA."
Saturday, May 12th, 6 a.m.

Reuter's London Telegrams from Poldhu, Cornwall, received on board this morning at 1 o'clock.

GREAT BRITAIN AND TURKEY.

Great Britain has sternly rejected the Turkish proposals regarding Tabah and has intimated to the Porte that nothing short of full satisfaction of the demands made will be acceptable.

THE NEW RUSSIAN PARLIAMENT.

The Duma opened with great pomp and ceremony in the Winter Palace. The speech of the Tsar promised to maintain the new Institutions in their entirety. Marked demonstrations are taking place throughout the Empire.

THE HAMBURG STRIKE.
SERIOUS CASUALTIES.

The mob of locked-out dock workmen at Hamburg attacked thirty English labourers and, in a pitched battle, two Englishmen were thrown into the river Elbe and eight others injured.

THE STRIKE IN ITALY.

The strike movement is spreading throughout Italy, and in some places collisions have occurred between the troops and the inhabitants. The strike, however, is not supported by the bulk of the population. In Rome the bystanders cheered the cavalry charging the strikers.

THE NATIVE RISING IN NATAL.

Natal is raising additional troops. Active operations have been begun against the rising in the interior. Many kraals have been fired and burned to the ground. Much sniping has taken place.

THE KAISER'S VISIT TO AUSTRIA.

The Kaiser's visit to Vienna is being greatly discussed, and many rumours are current as to the possibility of a fresh grouping of the Powers.

Associated Press Telegrams from Cape Cod, Mass., received on board this morning at 3 o'clock.

THE CASTELLANE DIVORCE SUIT.

At the hearing of the Castellane divorce case in Paris on Thursday, it was disclosed that there was no possibility or chance of reconciliation, the Countess insisting upon absolute divorce.

RAILROAD COLLISION.

A Lynchburg (Va.) telegram reports a collision on the Norfolk and Western Railroad. Four trainmen were killed and four injured.

THE BRITISH ULTIMATUM TO TURKEY

The term fixed by the British Ultimatum expires at midnight on Sunday. In official circles it is anticipated that the Porte will accept the British demands. In the event of the Sultan proving obdurate, however, active coercive measures will commence immediately upon the expiration of the period of grace.

WILSON'S VETO OF LITERACY TEST FOR IMMIGRANTS
January 28, 1915

> Presidents Cleveland, Taft and Wilson vetoed bills incorpor-
> ating a literacy test for immigrants as discriminatory.   This
> is President Wilson's message accompanying his veto of the
> Act of 1915.   In 1917 the Act was passed over his veto.

To the House of Representatives: It is with unaffected regret that
I find myself constrained by clear conviction to return this bill without
my signature.   Not only do I feel it to be a very serious matter to exercise the power of veto in any case, because it involves opposing the single
judgement of the President to the judgement of a majority of both Houses
of the Congress . . . but also because this particular bill is in so many
important respects admirable, well conceived, and desirable.   Its enactment into law would undoubtedly enhance the efficiency and improve the
methods of handling the important branch of the public service to which
it relates.   But candor and a sense of duty with regard to the responsibil-
ity so clearly imposed upon me by the Constitution in matters of legislation
leave me no choice but to dissent.

In two particulars of vital consequence this bill embodies a radical
departure from the traditional and long established policy of this country,
a policy in which our people have conceived the very character of their
Government to be expressed, the very mission and spirit of the Nation in
respect of its relations to the peoples of the world outside their borders.
It seeks to all but close entirely the gates of asylum which have always
been open to those who could find nowhere else the right and opportunity
of constitutional agitation for what they conceived to be the natural and
inalienable rights of men; and it excludes those to whom the opportunities
of elementary education have been denied, without regard to their character,
their purposes, or their natural capacity.

Restrictions like these, adopted earlier in our history as a Nation,
would very materially have altered the course and cooled the humane ardors
of our politics.   The right of political asylum has brought to this country
many a man of noble character and elevated purpose who was marked as an
outlaw in his own less fortunate land, and who has yet become an ornament
to our citizenship and to our public councils.   The children and compatriots
of these illustrious Americans must stand amazed to see the representatives of their Nation now resolved, in the fullness of our national strength
and at the maturity of our great institutions, to risk turning such men back
from our shores without test of quality or purpose.   It is difficult for me
to believe that the full effect of this feature of the bill was realized when
it was framed and adopted, and it is impossible for me to assent to it in the
form in which it is here cast.

The literacy test and the tests and restrictions which accompany it
constitute an even more radical change in the policy of the Nation.   Hitherto we have generously kept our doors open to all who were not unfitted by
reason of disease or incapacity for self-support or such personal records

and antecedents as were likely to make them a menace to our peace and order or to the wholesome and essential relationships of life. In this bill it is proposed to turn away from tests of character and of quality and impose tests which exclude and restrict; for the laws here embodied are not tests of quality or of character or of personal fitness, but tests of opportunity. Those who come seeking opportunity are not to be admitted unless they have already had one of the chief of the opportunities they seek, the opportunity of education. The object of such provisions is restriction, not selection.

If the people of this country have made up their minds to limit the number of immigrants by arbitrary tests and so reverse the policy of all the generations of Americans that have gone before them, it is their right to do so. I am their servant and have no license to stand in their way. But I do not believe that they have. I respectfully submit that no one can quote their mandate to that effect. Has any political party ever avowed a policy of restriction in this fundamental matter, gone to the country on it, and been commissioned to control its legislation? Does this bill rest upon the conscious and universal assent and desire of the American people? I doubt it. It is because I DOUBT IT THAT I make bold to dissent from it. I am willing to bide by the verdict, but not until it has been rendered. Let the platforms of parties speak out upon this policy and the people pronounce their wish. The matter is too fundamental to be settled otherwise.

I have no pride of opinion in this question. I am not foolish enough to profess to know the wishes and ideals of America better than the body of her chosen representatives know them. I only want instruction direct from those whose fortunes with ours, and all men's are involved.

The history of criminal justice in America is not complete without the famous trial of Sacco and Vanzetti. Famous jurists still have grave misgivings about a possible miscarriage of justice. Vanzetti's statement, given shortly before his execution, follows:

Yes. What I say is that I am innocent, not only of the Braintree crime but also of the Bridgewater crime. That I am not only innocent of these two crimes, but in all my life I have never stole and I have never killed and I have never spilled blood. That is what I want to say. And it is not all. Not only am I innocent of these two crimes, not only in all my life I have never stole, never killed, never spilled blood, but I have struggled all my life, since I began to reason, to eliminate crime from the earth.

Everybody that knows these two arms knows very well that I did not need to go in between the street and kill a man to take the money. I can live with my two arms and live well. But besides that, I can live even without work with my arm for other people. I have had plenty of chance to live independently and to live what the world conceives to be a higher life than not to gain our bread with the sweat of our brow . . . .

Well, I want to reach a little point farther, and it is this---that not only have I not been trying to steal in Bridgewater, not only have I not been in Braintree to steal and kill and have never steal or kill or spilt blood in all my life, not only have I struggled hard against crimes, but I have refused myself the commodity or glory of life, the pride of life of a good position because in my consideration it is not right to exploit man . . . .

Now, I should say that I am not only innocent of all these things, not only have I never committed a real crime in my life---though some sins, but not crimes---not only have I struggled all my life to eliminate crimes that the official law and the official moral condemns, but also the crime that the official moral and the official law sanctions and sanctifies,---the exploitation and the oppression of the man by the man, and if there is a reason why you in a few minutes can doom me, it is this reason and none else.

I beg your pardon. There is the more good man I ever cast my eyes upon since I lived, a man that will last and will grow always more near and more dear to the people, as far as into the heart of the people, so long as admiration for goodness and for sacrifice will last. I mean Eugene Debs . . . . He know, and not only he but every man of understanding in the world, not only in this country but also in the other countries, men that we have provided a certain amount of a record of the times, they all stick with us, the flower of mankind of Europe, the better writers, the greatest thinkers, of Europe, have pleaded in our favor. The scientists, the greatest scientists, the greatest statesmen of Europe, have pleaded in our favor. The people of foreign nations have pleaded in our favor.

Is it possible that only a few on the jury, only two or three men, who would condemn their mother for worldly honor and for earthly fortune; is

it possible that they are right against what the world, the whole world has
say it is wrong and that I know that it is wrong?   If there is one that I should
know it, if it is right or if it is wrong, it is I and this man.   You see it is
seven years that we are in jail.   What we have suffered during those years
no human tongue can say, and yet you see me before you, not trembling you
see me looking you in your eyes straight, not blushing, not changing color,
not ashamed or in fear . . . .

We have proved that there could not have been another Judge on the
face of the earth more prejudiced and more cruel than you have been against
us.   We have proved that.   Still they refuse the new trial.   We know, and
you know in your heart, that you have been against us from the very beginning, before you see us.   Before you see us you already know that we were
radicals, that we were underdogs, that we were the enemy of the institution
that you can believe in good faith in their goodness---I don't want to condemn that---and that it was easy on the time of the first trial to get a verdict of guiltiness.

We know that you have spoke yourself and have spoke your hostility
against us, and your despisement against us with friends of yours on the
train, at the University Club, of Boston, on the Golf Club of Worcester,
Massachusetts.   I am sure that if the people who know all what you say
against us would have the civil courage to take the stand, maybe your Honor
----I am sorry to say this because you are an old man, and I have an old
father---but maybe you would be beside us in good justice at this time.

When you sentenced me at the Plymouth trial you say, to the best
part of my memory, of my good faith, that crimes were in accordance with
my principle,---something of that sort---and you take off one charge, if I
remember it exactly, from the jury.   The jury was so violent against me
that they found me guilty of both charges, because there were only two. . .

We were tried during a time that has now passed into history.   I
mean by that, a time when there was hysteria of resentment and hate against
the people of our principles, against the foreigner, against slackers, and
it seems to me---rather, I am positive, that both you and Mr. Katzmann
has done all what it were in your power in order to work out, in order to
agitate still more the passion of the juror, the prejudice of the juror,
against us . . . .

Well, I have already say that I not only am not guilty of these crimes,
but I never commit a crime in my life, --- I have never steal and I have
never kill and I have never spilt blood, and I have fought against the crime,
and I have fought and I have sacrificed myself even to eliminate the crimes
that the law and the church legitimate and sanctify.

This is what I say: I would not wish to a dog or to a snake, to the
most low and misfortunate creature on the earth---I would not wish to
any of them what I have had to suffer for things that I am not guilty of.
But my conviction is that I have suffered for things that I am guilty of.
I am suffering because I am a radical and indeed I am a radical; I have
suffered because I was an Italian, and indeed I am an Italian; I have suffer-

ed more for my family and for my beloved than for myself; but I am so convinced to be right that if you could execute me two times, and if I could be reborn two other times, I would live again to do what I have done already. I have finished.   Thank you.

EINSTEIN'S LETTER TO ROOSEVELT

Enrico Fermi had suggested that the United States government concern and involve itself very seriously in the matter of nuclear chain reaction in the interest of national defense. Albert Einstein saw the urgency of the matter and asked President Franklin D. Roosevelt to become immediately interested. His letter to the President follows.

Albert Einstein
Old Grove Rd.
Nassau Point
Peconic, Long Island

August 2nd, 1939

F. D. Roosevelt,
President of the United States,
White House
Washington, D. C.

Sir:

Some recent work by E. Fermi and L. Szilard, which has been communicated to me in manuscript, leads me to expect that the element uranium may be turned into a new and important source of energy in the immediate future. Certain aspects of the situation which has arisen seem to call for watchfulness and, if necessary, quick action on the part of the Administration. I believe therefore that it is my duty to bring to your attention the following facts and recommendations:

In the course of the last four months it has been made probable through the work of Joliot in France as well as Fermi and Szilard in America - that it may become possible to set up a nuclear chain reaction in a large mass of uranium, by which vast amounts of power and large quantities of new radium-like elements would be generated. Now it appears almost certain that this could be achieved in the immediate future.

This new phenomenon would also lead to the construction of bombs, and it is conceivable - though much less certain - that extremely powerful bombs of a new type may thus be constructed. A singel bomb of this type, carried by boat and exploded in a port, might very well destroy the whole port together with some of the surrounding territory. However, such bombs might very well prove to be too heavy for transportation by air.

The United States has only very poor ores of uranium in moderate quantities. There is some good ore in Canada and the former Czechoslovakia, while the most important source of uranium is Belgian Congo.

In view of this situation you may think it desirable to have some permanent contact maintained between the Administration and the group of physicists working on chain reactions in America. One possible way of achieving this might be for you to entrust with this task a person who has your confidence and who could perhaps serve in an inofficial capacity. His task might comprise the following:

a) to approach Government Departments, keep them informed of the further development, and put forward recommendations for Government action, giving particular attention to the problem of securing a supply of uranium ore for the United States;

b) to speed up the experimental work, which is at present being carried on within the limits of the budgets of University laboratories, by providing funds, if such funds be required, through his contacts with private persons who are willing to make contributions for this cause, and perhaps also by obtaining the co-operation of industrial laboratories which have the necessary equipment.

I understand that Germany has actually stopped the sale of uranium from the Czechoslovakian mines which she has taken over. That she should have taken such early action might perhaps be understood on the ground that the son of the German Under-Secretary of State, von Weizsacker, is attached to the Kaiser-Wilhelm-Institut in Berlin where some of the American work on uranium is now being repeated.

Yours very truly,

(Albert Einstein)

Public Law 89-236
89th Congress, H. R. 2580
October 3, 1965

An Act

To amend the Immigration and Nationality Act, and for other purposes.

Be it enacted by the Senate and House of Representatives of the United States of America in Congress assembled, That section 201 of the Immigration and Nationality Act (66 Stat. 175; 8 U.S.C. 1151) be amended to read as follows:

"SEC. 201. (a) Exclusive of special immigrants defined in section 101(a)(27), and of the immediate relatives of United States citizens specified in subsection (b) of this section, the number of aliens who may be issued immigrant visas or who may otherwise acquire the status of an alien lawfully admitted to the United States for permanent residence, or who may, pursuant to section 203(a)(7) enter conditionally, (i) shall not in any of the first three quarters of any fiscal year exceed a total of 45,000 and (ii) shall not in any fiscal year exceed a total of 170,000.

"(b) The 'immediate relatives' referred to in subsection (a) of this section shall mean the children, spouses, and parents of a citizen of the United States: *Provided,* That in the case of parents, such citizen must be at least twenty-one years of age. The immediate relatives specified in this subsection who are otherwise qualified for admission as immigrants shall be admitted as such, without regard to the numerical limitations in this Act.

"(c) During the period from July 1, 1965, through June 30, 1968, the annual quota of any quota area shall be the same as that which existed for that area on June 30, 1965. The Secretary of State shall, not later than on the sixtieth day immediately following the date of enactment of this subsection and again on or before September 1, 1966, and September 1, 1967, determine and proclaim the amount of quota numbers which remain unused at the end of the fiscal year ending on June 30, 1965, June 30, 1966, and June 30, 1967, respectively, and are available for distribution pursuant to subsection (d) of this section.

"(d) Quota numbers not issued or otherwise used during the previous fiscal year, as determined in accordance with subsection (c) hereof, shall be transferred to an immigration pool. Allocation of numbers from the pool and from national quotas shall not together exceed in any fiscal year the numerical limitations in subsection (a) of this section. The immigration pool shall be made available to immigrants otherwise admissible under the provisions of this Act who are unable to obtain prompt issuance of a preference visa due to oversubscription of their quotas, or subquotas as determined by the Secretary of State. Visas and conditional entries shall be allocated from the immigration pool within the percentage limitations and in the order of priority specified in section 203 without regard to the quota to which the alien is chargeable.

"(e) The immigration pool and the quotas of quota areas shall terminate June 30, 1968. Thereafter immigrants admissible under the provisions of this Act who are subject to the numerical limitations of subsection (a) of this section shall be admitted in accordance with the percentage limitations and in the order of priority specified in section 203."

SEC. 2. Section 202 of the Immigration and Nationality Act (66 Stat. 175; 8 U.S.C. 1152) is amended to read as follows:

"(a) No person shall receive any preference or priority or be discriminated against in the issuance of an immigrant visa because of his race, sex, nationality, place of birth, or place of residence, except as specifically provided in section 101(a)(27), section 201(b), and section 203: *Provided,* That the total number of immigrant visas and the number of conditional entries made available to natives of any single foreign state under paragraphs (1) through (8) of section 203(a) shall not exceed 20,000 in any fiscal year: *Provided further*, That the foregoing proviso shall not operate to reduce the number of immigrants who may be admitted under the quota of any quota area before June 30, 1968.

"(b) Each independent country, self-governing dominion, mandated territory, and territory under the international trusteeship system of the United Nations, other than the United States and its outlying possessions shall be treated as a separate foreign state for the purposes of the numerical limitation set forth in the proviso to subsection (a) of this section when approved by the Secretary of State. All other inhabited lands shall be attributed to a foreign state specified by the Secretary of State. For the purposes of this Act the foreign state to which an immigrant is chargeable shall be determined by birth within such foreign state except that (1) an alien child, when accompanied by his alien parent or parents, may be charged to the same foreign state as the accompanying parent or of either accompanying parent if such parent has received or would be qualified for an immigrant visa, if necessary to prevent the separation of the child from the accompanying parent or parents, and if the foreign state to which such parent has been or would be chargeable has not exceeded the numerical limitation set forth in the proviso to subsection (a) of this section for that fiscal year; (2) if an alien is chargeable to a different foreign state from that of his accompanying spouse, the foreign state to which such alien is chargeable may, if necessary to prevent the separation of husband and wife, be determined by the foreign state of the accompanying spouse, if such spouse has received or would be qualified for an immigrant visa and if the foreign state to which such spouse has been or would be chargeable has not exceeded the numerical limitation set forth in the proviso to subsection (a) of this section for that fiscal year; (3) an alien born in the United States shall be considered as having been born in the country of which he is a citizen or subject, or if he is not a citizen or subject of any country then in the last foreign country in which he had his residence as determined by the consular officer; (4) an alien born within any foreign state in which neither of his parents was born and in which neither of his parents had a residence at the time of such alien's birth may be charged to the foreign state of either parent.

"(c) Any immigrant born in a colony or other component or dependent area of a foreign state unless a special immigrant as provided in section 101(a) (27) or an immediate relative of a United States citizen as specified in section 201(b), shall be chargeable, for the purpose of limitation set forth in section 202(a), to the foreign state, except that the number of persons born in any such colony or other component or dependent area overseas from the foreign state chargeable to the foreign state in any one fiscal year shall not exceed 1 per centum of the maximum number of immigrant visas available to such foreign state.

"(d) In the case of any change in the territorial limits of foreign states, the Secretary of State shall, upon recognition of such change, issue appropriate instructions to all diplomatic and consular offices."

SEC. 3. Section 203 of the Immigration and Nationality Act (66 Stat. 175; 8 U.S.C. 1153) is amended to read as follows:

"SEC. 203. (a) Aliens who are subject to the numerical limitations specified in section 201(a) shall be allotted visas or their conditional entry authorized, as the case may be, as follows:

"(1) Visas shall be first made available, in a number not to exceed 20 per centum of the number specified in section 201(a) (ii), to qualified immigrants who are the unmarried sons or daughters of citizens of the United States.

"(2) Visas shall next be made available, in a number not to exceed 20 per centum of the number specified in section 201(a)(ii), plus any visas not required for the classes specified in paragraph (1), to qualified immigrants who are the spouses, unmarried sons or unmarried daughters of an alien lawfully admitted for permanent residence.

"(3) Visas shall next be made available, in a number not to exceed 10 per centum of the number specified in section 201(a)(ii), to qualified immigrants who are members of the professions, or who because of their exceptional ability in the sciences or the arts will substantially benefit prospectively the national economy, cultural interests, or welfare of the United States.

"(4) Visas shall next be made available, in a number not to exceed 10 per centum of the number specified in section 201(a)(ii), plus any visas not required for the classes specified in paragraphs (1) through (3), to qualified immigrants who are the married sons or the married daughters of citizens of the United States.

"(5) Visas shall next be made available, in a number not to exceed 24 per centum of the number specified in section 201(a)(ii), plus any visas not required for the classes specified in paragraphs (1) through (4), to qualified immigrants who are the brothers or sisters of citizens of the United States.

"(6) Visas shall next be made available, in a number not to exceed 10 per centum of the number specified in section 201(a)(ii), to qualified immigrants who are capable of performing specified skilled or unskilled labor, not of a temporary or seasonal nature, for which a shortage of employable and willing persons exists in the United States.

"(7) Conditional entries shall next be made available by the Attorney General, pursuant to such regulations as he may prescribe and in a number not to exceed 6 per centum of the number specified in section 201(a)(ii), to aliens who satisfy an Immigration and Naturalization Service officer at an examination in any non-Communist or non-Communist-dominated country, (A) that (i) because of persecution or fear of persecution on account of race, religion, or political opinion they have fled (I) from any Communist or Communist-dominated country or area, or (II) from any country within the general area of the Middle East, and (ii) are unable or unwilling to return to such country or area on account of race, religion, or political opinion, and (iii) are not nationals of the countries or areas in which their application for conditional entry is made; or (B) that they are persons uprooted by catastrophic natural calamity as defined by the President who are unable to return to their usual place of abode. For the purpose of the foregoing the term 'general area of the Middle East' means the area between and including (1) Libya on the west, (2) Turkey on the north, (3) Pakistan on the east, and (4) Saudi Arabia and Ethiopia on the south: *Provided*, That immigrant visas in a number not exceeding one-half the number specified in this paragraph may be made available, in lieu of conditional entries of a like number, to such aliens who have been continuously physically present in the United States for a period of at least two years prior to application for adjustment of status.

"(8) Visas authorized in any fiscal year, less those required for issuance to the classes specified in paragraphs (1) through (6) and less the number of conditional entries and visas made available pursuant to paragraph (7), shall be made available to other qualified immigrants strictly in the chronological order in which they qualify. Waiting lists of applicants shall be maintained in accordance with regulations prescribed by the Secretary of State. No immigrant visa shall be issued to a nonpreference immigrant under this paragraph, or to an immigrant with a preference under paragraph (3) or (6) of this subsection, until the consular officer is in receipt of a determination made by the Secretary of Labor pursuant to the provisions of section 212(a)(14).

"(9) A spouse or child as defined in section 101(b)(1)(A), (B), (C), (D), or (E) shall, if not otherwise entitled to an immigrant status and the immediate issuance of a visa or to conditional entry under paragraphs (1) through (8), be entitled to the same status, and the same order of consideration provided in subsection (b); if accompanying, or following to join, his spouse or parent.

"(b) In considering applications for immigrant visas under subsection (a) consideration shall be given to applicants in the order in which the classes of which they are members are listed in subsection (a).

"(c) Immigrant visas issued pursuant to paragraphs (1) through (6) of subsection (a) shall be issued to eligible immigrants in the order in which a petition in behalf of each such immigrant is filed with the Attorney General as provided in section 204.

"(d) Every immigrant shall be presumed to be a nonpreference immigrant until he establishes to the satisfaction of the consular officer and the immigration officer that he is entitled to a preference status under paragraphs (1) through (7) of subsection (a), or to a special immigrant status under section 101(a)(27), or that he is an immediate relative of a United States citizen as specified in section 201(b). In the case of any alien claiming in his application for an immigrant visa to be an immediate relative of a United States citizen as specified in section 201(b) or to be entitled to preference immigrant status under paragraphs (1) through (6) of subsection (a), the consular officer shall not grant such status until he has been authorized to do so as provided by section 204.

"(e) For the purposes of carrying out his responsibilities in the orderly administration of this section, the Secretary of State is authorized to make reasonable estimates of the anticipated numbers of visas to be issued during any quarter of any fiscal year within each of the categories of subsection (a), and to rely upon such estimates in authorizing the issuance of such visas. The Secretary of State, in his discretion, may terminate the registration on a waiting list of any alien who fails to evidence his continued intention to apply for a visa in such manner as may be by regulation prescribed.

"(f) The Attorney General shall submit to the Congress a report containing complete and detailed statement of facts in the case of each alien who conditionally entered the United States pursuant to subsection (a)(7) of this section. Such reports shall be submitted on or before January 15 and June 15 of each year.

"(g) Any alien who conditionally entered the United States as a refugee, pursuant to subsection (a)(7) of this section, whose conditional entry has not been terminated by the Attorney General pursuant to such regulations as he may prescribe, who has been in the United States for at least two years, and who has not acquired permanent residence, shall forthwith return or be returned to the custody of the Immigration and Naturalization Service and shall thereupon be inspected and examined for admission into the United States, and his case dealt with in accordance with the provisions of sections 235, 236, and 237 of this Act.

"(h) Any alien who, pursuant to subsection (g) of this section, is found, upon inspection by the immigration officer or after hearing before a special inquiry officer, to be admissible as an immigrant under this Act at the time of his inspection and examination, except for the fact that he was not and is not in possession of the documents required by section 212(a)(20), shall be regarded as lawfully admitted to the United States for permanent residence as of the date of his arrival."

90TH CONGRESS
1ST SESSION

H. R. 2372

IN THE HOUSE OF REPRESENTATIVES

JANUARY 16, 1967

Mr. RODINO introduced the following bill; which was referred to the Committee on the Judiciary

A BILL

Declaring October 12 to be a legal holiday.

1   *Be it enacted by the Senate and House of Representa-*

2 *tives of the United States of America in Congress assembled,*

3 That the 12th day of October of each year, to be hereafter

4 celebrated and known as "Columbus Day", is hereby

5 declared to be a legal holiday of the same character as the

6 1st day of January, the 22d day of February, the 30th day

7 of May, the 4th day of July, the first Monday of September,

8 the 11th day of November, the fourth Thursday of Novem-

9 ber, and Christmas Day.

Senate Concurrent Resolution No. 70

Resolved by the Senate (the House of Representatives concurring), That the Joint Committee on the Library is authorized and directed to procure a marble bust of Constantino Brumidi, and to cause such bust to be placed in the corridor, known as the Brumidi corridor, on the first floor of the Senate wing of the Capitol.

SEC. 2. Expenses incurred by the Joint Committee on the Library in carrying out this concurrent resolution, which shall not exceed $2,500, shall be paid out of the contingent fund of the Senate on vouchers approved by the chairman of the Joint Committee.

Passed the Senate March 25, 1966.

Attest:

Secretary.

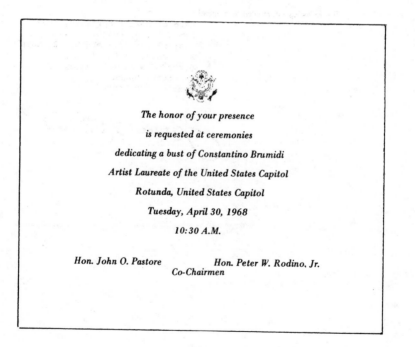

The honor of your presence

is requested at ceremonies

dedicating a bust of Constantino Brumidi

Artist Laureate of the United States Capitol

Rotunda, United States Capitol

Tuesday, April 30, 1968

10:30 A.M.

Hon. John O. Pastore   *Hon. Peter W. Rodino, Jr.*
Co-Chairmen

OFFICIAL RECORD OF THE BIRTHPLACE
OF ALFRED E. SMITH'S GRANDFATHER

MUNICIPAL ARCHIVES AND RECORDS CENTER

23 PARK ROW

NEW YORK, N.Y. 10038

Date.........October 13, 1970......

THIS IS TO CERTIFY THAT a search was made in the records

of ......Deaths................ in the Borough of ...Manhattan......................

City of New York for the calendar year/s ....1859...

The following information was found:

Date of Death: April 10, 1859
Name: Smith, Emanuel
Age: 51 years, 2 months, 23 days
Residence: 31 Hamilton
Place of Nativity: Italy
Cemetery: Union
Sexton: Not Listed

James Richards
DIRECTOR

ON THE CARE OF MIGRANTS

On August 22, 1969, Pope Paul VI issued his <u>Instruction on the Pastoral Care of People Who Migrate.</u> This was an updating of the classical mandate of Pius XII known as <u>Exsul Familia</u> in 1952. The latter was known as the Church's "Magna Charta for Migrants". It was a luminous testimony of the loving care of the Church for those who had left their homeland. Excerpts of the newer document give its spirit and tone.

. . . .

2. Unity of the Human Family

A new and broader thrust towards unification of all peoples and of the whole world arises from this movement of peoples. In this "God's Spirit, who with a marvelous providence directs the unfolding of time and renews the face of the earth," is easily perceived.

Migrations, which favor and promote mutual understanding and cooperation on the part of all, give witness to and promote the unity of the human family, and confirm that communion of brotherhood among peoples "in which each party is at the same time a giver and a receiver."

3. Problems Inherent to Migration

But even acknowledging as accurate the above reasons in favor of migrations, one cannot deny that there are at the same time many hazards and difficulties, often amplified---or at least not lessened---by the great size of the migrations. Social relations indeed are multiplying today, yet without always promoting the corresponding maturity of the individual and that which truly pertains to the person. From this arise many difficulties and sufferings, of which "man is at once a cause and the victim."

One should call to mind particularly the tensions due to economic inequality, the conflicts proceeding from differences of mentality and tradition, and "with respect to the fundamental rights of the person, every type of discrimination, whether social or cultural, whether based on sex, race, color, social condition, language, or origin," and finally historical prejudices and political or ideological intolerance.

. . . .

5. Respect for the Fundamental Rights of the Human Person

Man "whole and entire, body and soul" is the proper object of the Church's pastoral concern. When the care of souls is to be adapted to the needs of the times, it seems most proper to recall the primary and fundamental rights of the human person again and again, in order that persons

67

who govern may recognize and protect those rights, and that migrant people themselves may realize that they are involved in the duties of citizens and of the community, and that they may consider their duties carefully.

6. The Right of Having a Homeland

It flows from the social nature of man that he is a citizen of some State or homeland, to which he is bound, not only by the rights of descent and blood, but by spiritual and cultural bonds.

The primary and fundamental rights of man are violated when either individual men or ethnic groups are deprived of their home and homeland because of different race or religion or for any other reason.

7. The Right of Emigrating

Men have a native right of using the material and spiritual goods which "allow . . . relatively thorough and ready access to their own fulfillment." But where a State which suffers from poverty combined with great population cannot supply such use of goods to its inhabitants, or where the State places conditions which offend human dignity, people possess a right to emigrate, to select a new home in foreign lands, and to seek conditions of life worthy of man.

This right pertains not only to individual persons, but to whole families as well. Therefore "in decisions affecting migrants their right to live together as a family [is to be] safeguarded," with consideration of the needs of family housing, the education of children, working conditions, social insurance, and taxes.

Public authorities unjustly deny the rights of human persons if they block or impede emigration or immigration except where grave requirements of the common good, considered objectively, demand it.

. . . .

11. The Right of Keeping One's Native Tongue and Spiritual Heritage

Migrating people carry with them their own mentality, their own language, their own culture, and their own religion. All of these things are parts of a certain spiritual heritage of opinions, traditions and culture which will perdure outside the homeland. Let it be prized highly everywhere.

Not least in its right to consideration is the mother tongue of emigrant people, by which they express their mentality, thoughts, culture and spiritual life.

Since these last are the natural media for knowing and opening the inner man, the care of migrating people will indeed bear fruit if it is carried out by persons who know them all well [i.e., the mentality, thoughts, culture, and spiritual life] and who are fully proficient in the people's language. Thus is confirmed the already-obvious advantage of caring for people who migrate through priests of their own language, and this as long as usefulness indicates.

AWARD WINNERS

In society, rewards given are many because the talent of man is great and he has made, produced, found, discovered or attained almost the impossible. The Italians, gifted by nature, have shared liberally in the awards. Just a few representative Italian-American names follow. In many instances, the persons listed were honored by multiple awards; only one or two, however, might be given here for practicality purposes.

ABETTI, Pier Antonio

Electrical engineer.
1955 – Coffin Award.
1956 – International Montefiore Prize.

CARUSO, Dennis

Photographer.
1970 – Page One Awards for Spot News Photography, N.Y. Daily News.

CASSINI, Count Igor Loiewski (Cholly Knickerbocker)

Newspaper Columnist.
1949 – Freedom Foundation, Gold Medal Award for achievement in bringing about better understanding of the American way of life.

CIOFFI, Lou

Newscaster.
1970 – Overseas Press Club Award.

CROCCO, Luigi Mario

Physicist.
1971 – James W. Wyld Propulsion Award for achievement in the development of rocket propulsion systems.

ESPOSITO, John

Conservationist.
1970 – National Wildlife Federation Award; Air conservation.

FEDERICI, William

Journalist.
1970 – George Polk Memorial Award for Metropolitan Reporting, N. Y. Daily News.

FERMI, Enrico

Scientist.
1938 – Nobel Prize in Physics.

69

FISCHETTI, John

Cartoonist.
1969 - Pulitzer Prize Award for the best example of a newspaper cartoonist's work; Chicago Daily News.

FRASCA, John Anthony

Newspaperman.
1956 - Best Writing of the Year Award, Philadelphia Press Association.
1966 - Pulitzer Prize for outstanding example of local reporting, Tampa (Florida) Tribune.

GASPARO, Oronzo

Painter.
Artists of America Award (First Prize) for his watercolor "Caravan."

JOIO, Dello Norman

Composer.
1957 - Pulitzer Prize Award for his composition of "Meditations on Ecclesiastes."

LUCIONI, Luigi

Artist.
1928 - Tiffany Medal.
1929 - Allied Artists Medal of Honor.
1946 - Purchase Prize Library of Congress.

LURIA, Salvador E.

Biologist.
1969 - Nobel Prize in Physiology and Medicine.

MENOTTI, Gian-Carlo

Composer.
1950 - Pulitzer Prize for his composition of "The Consul."
1955 - Pulitzer Prize for his composition of "The Saint of Bleeker Street."

PERSICHETTI, Vincent

Composer.
1958-1959 - Guggenheim Fellowship award.
1962 - Lincoln Center.

PETRI, Elio and PIRRO, Ugo

Authors.
1970 - Edgar Award in Literature for the best mystery movie: Investigation of a Citizen above Suspicion.

PIEROTTI, John   Cartoonist.
                                1970 - Society of the Silurians
                                         Award for Journalistic
                                         Achievement.

                                1971 - Page One Award for the best
                                         editorial cartoon, New York
                                         Post.

PETRILLI, Carl J.   Architectural designer.
                                1971 - Bard Award for his design of
                                         the Graduate Center Mall of
                                         City University of New York.

RIZZO, Frank L.   Police Commissioner, Philadelphia,
                                Pennsylvania.
                                1970 - Freedom Foundation Awards -
                                         National Recognition.

SANTORA, Philip Joseph   Feature writer.
                                1956 - Polk Memorial Award for best
                                         metropolitan reporting.
                                1959 - Pulitzer Prize for internation-
                                         al reporting.
                                1959 - Page One Award for series on
                                         Cuban revolution.
                                1960 - Silurian Award for best public
                                         service series on Castro's
                                         Cuba.

SEGRÈ, Emilio G.   Scientist.
                                1959 - Nobel Prize in Physics.

VINCIGUERRA, John V.   Scientist.
                                1971 - Atomic Energy Commission
                                         Award Distinguished Service.

Italy and Italians have been prominent in the commercial world from the times of the famous City States of northern Italy and the formation therefrom of the Law Merchant, the basis of international commercial law. Since the United States is the adopted home of so many Italians, it is only natural that Italians should make their grateful contribution to the great business enterprise of America.

These names and firms are merely representative of the literally thousands of such industrialists and industries, chosen at randam, throughout the United States.

INDUSTRIALISTS

CASTRO, Bernard

Manufacturer of the famous Castro Convertible. Multimillionaire; head of the greatest company of its kind in America.

CUNEO, Francesco

Came to America around 1890. Introduced and made Italian chestnuts a popular item of the American diet. He was one of the wealthiest Italians in New York.

CUNEO, John

President of Cuneo Press, one of the greatest printing firms in the world. Established originally in Chicago as Cuneo Henneberry Company (later Cuneo Press, Inc.) in 1924, presently located in Philadelphia, Pa., with offices in New York.

DE NUNZIO, Ralph Dwight

Investment banker; Director, Ralwin Realty Corp. and of Dreyfus Offshore Trust; Vice-Chairman of the Board of the New York Stock Exchange since 1969.

IOCOCCA, Lido (Lee) Anthony

Automobile manufacturer, President of Ford North American Automobile Operations.

MARUSI, Augustine

President of the Chemical Division of the Borden Company since 1960 and President of the Borden Company since 1967.

72

PETRILLO, James C.

Former President of the Chicago Federation of Musicians and of the American Federation of Musicians; now Chairman of the Civil Rights Department; past Vice-President of the American Federation of Labor.

POLI, Sebastiano

Businessman who gathered pennies as he cranked a hand organ with a monkey dancing. He established a chain of theatres which he sold to William Fox for thirty million dollars.

RAGGIO, Olga

Art curator, Chairman of the Metropolitan Museum's Department of Western European Arts.

RIZZOLI, Angelo

Italian publisher and film producer in Milan. His communications empire, which includes Italy's popular weekly magazine "OGGI", is said to have an annual gross income of more than fifty million dollars. International publisher.

SARDI, Melchiorre Pio Vincenzo

Opened Sardi's Restaurant in New York in 1922. Probably unmatched in America as a rendezvous for luminaries of stage, screen, radio and television.

TERENZIO, Peter Bernard

Hospital Administrator. Commissioner, Department of Hospitals, New York City, from 1961 to 1965.

TRAPANI, Antonio

Rich merchant and businessman who was the first foreigner to become a naturalized American citizen according to the regulations established by the Constitution.

TUCCI, Oscar

In 1916 became the new owner of the famous Delmonico's Restaurant in the financial district of New York City; now known as Oscar's Delmonico Restaurant.

VISCARDI, Henry, Jr.

Business executive and rehabilitation specialist. Established JOB (Just One Break), an employment agency for amputees and victims of crippling diseases. Author of Give us the Tools, 1959; Laughter in the Lonely Night, 1961; and A Letter to Jimmy, 1962.

(Foreign and domestic products.)

FIRM	LOCATION	PRODUCTS
ANTOGNOLI, JOSEPH & COMPANY	Chicago, Illinois	Olive oil, cheese, etc.
BAZZINI, A. L. CO., INC.	New York, N. Y.	Assorted nuts, Brand: Bazzini
BERIO IMPORTING CORPORATION	New York, N. Y.	Olive oil & vinegar, Brands: Filippo Berio, Callisto Francesconi, Extra I
BOCCE SUPPLY COMPANY	Buffalo, N. Y.	Bocce balls and supplies
BRIONE'S & CO., INC.	Bronx, N. Y.	Wines, Brand: BANO
BRIOSCHI, ACHILLE & COMPANY, INC.	Fairlawn, N. J.	Tartaric acid, Brand: Brioschi
BUITONI FOODS CORPORATION	So. Hackensack, N.J.	Macaroni and related products. Brand: Buitoni
CASTRO CONVERT-IBLE	New Hyde Park, N. Y.	Convertible furniture
CORTINA SKI COMPANY, INC.	New York, N. Y.	Sportswear, skis, etc. Brand: Cortina
D'AGOSTINO, EDWIN D.	Providence, R. I.	Housewares, Brands: Comluy, Vian, Pavese, Rosa Enzo.
DE ROSA FOOD PRODUCTS	Little Ferry, N. J.	Tomatoes, olive oil, etc. Brand: Pope
FEDERAL STORAGE WAREHOUSES	Newark, N. J.	Warehousing and distribution depots.
FERRARA FOODS & CONFECTIONS	New York, N. Y.	Food & confections, Brands: Ferrara, Valpa, Dulciora, Alemagna
GIULIETTI ACCORDION CORPORATION	New York, N. Y.	Musical instruments, Brands: Giulietti, JG. Bassetti

FIRM	LOCATION	PRODUCTS
GEMIGNANI, ENRICO	St. Clair Shores, Michigan	Marble and granite
GHIRADELLI CHOCO-LATE COMPANY	San Francisco, California	Chocolates
GUCCI SHOPS, INC.	New York, N. Y.	Leather goods, Brand: Gucci
ICCO CHEESE CO., INC.	Brooklyn, N. Y.	Cheese and spices
IOFFREDO, CARLO-ITALWINE IMPORT CO., INC.	Winter Park, Fla.	Wines and Liqueurs
LA CASA DEL TESORO	Los Angeles, California	Jewelry and folk art
LA FARA IMPORTING COMPANY	Philadelphia, Pa.	Macaroni, Brand: La Fara
V. LA ROSA & SONS, LTD.	Westbury, N. Y.	Macaroni & related products, Brand: La Rosa
LOCATELLI, INC.	Stamford, Conn.	Cheese, Brand: Locatelli
LORENZONI, FELIX STUDIO, INC.	Greenwich, Conn.	Architectural marble works for churches, statues, etc. Brand: Giuseppe Lorenzoni
MAZZOLI COFFEE INC.	Brooklyn, N. Y.	Coffee brewing devices. Brands: Stella, Record Bianchi, Quick Mill
MAZZOLINI ART-CRAFT COMPANY	Cleveland, Ohio	Marble statuary.
MONDADORI PUBLISHING COM-PANY, INC.	New York, N. Y.	Books and magazines, Brands: Epoca, Arianna, Panorama, Confidenze, Bolero
NICCOLINI, INC.	Fort Lauderdale, Florida	Antiques
OLIVETTI CORP-ORATION OF AMERICA	New York, N. Y.	Business machines

FIRM	LOCATION	PRODUCTS
OSSOLA, J. CO., INC.	Totowa, N. J.	Tomatoes, tomato paste, Brand: Torino
PAOLI, GINO	Clifton, N. J.	Knitwear, Brands: Gino Paoli, Piccolino, Ecco, Andiamo, Piccolo
PASTENE & CO., INC.	New York, N. Y.	Olive oil, tomatoes, etc. Brands: Pastene, Pasco, Bue, Ovis, ,luce, Pagliaccio, La Napolitana, Piedigrotta
PICCINI, ANTONIO & Son	Brooklyn, N. Y.	Olive oil, tomatoes, mineral waters, etc. Brands: Tana, Mare Chiare
PICCOLI, R. S. - PAGLIERI PARFUMS, INC.	Williamsville, N. Y.	Colognes for men & women. Brands: Ambrato, Felce Azzurra, Paradiso, Cologne for Men.
PIETROBELLI, CARLO, INC.	Miami, Florida	Gifts, housewares and coffeemakers
PIRELLI TIRE CORPORATION	New York, N. Y.	Tires for all vehicles, Brand: Pirelli
RIMOLDI MFG. COMPANY OF AMERICA, INC.	Reading, Pa.	Industrial sewing machines and sewing machine parts. Brand: Rimoldi
RIZZOLI INTERNATIONAL BOOKSTORE	New York, N. Y.	International publishers and retail bookshop.
ROMA FURNITURE Co., Inc.	New York, N. Y.	Furniture
SAVINELLI PIPES OF AMERICA	Saddle Brook, N. J.	Briar pipes and no-nik filter cigarette holders. Brands: Savinelli Golden Jubilee, Punto Oro, Savinelli Capri, Savinelli De Luxe Milano & Sherwood Rock Briars
STELLO D'ORO BISCUIT CO., INC.	Bronx, N. Y.	Biscuit and cookie bakers, Brand: Stella D'Oro

ITALIAN-AMERICAN ORGANIZATIONS

Business and Civic	Founded	Location
American Committee on Italian Migration	1952	New York, N. Y.
American Justinian Society of Jurists	1966	Chicago, Ill.
Brooklyn Diocesan Migration Office	1971	Brooklyn, N. Y.
Columbian Lawyers' Association	1951	Queens, N. Y.
Columbian Lawyers' Association	1961	Brooklyn, N. Y.
Columbian Lawyers' Association, First Judicial Department	1955	Bronx Co., N. Y.
Congress of Italian American Organizations, Inc.	1966	New York, N. Y.
Italian American Chamber of Commerce of Michigan		Detroit, Mich.
Italian American Chamber of Commerce of the Pacific Coast		San Francisco, Calif.
Italian American Community Council of South Brooklyn	1971	Brooklyn, N. Y.
Italian American Professional and Businessmen's Association	1932	Brooklyn, N. Y.
Italian American War Veterans of the U. S.	1932	Syracuse, N. Y.
Italian American Labor Council	1941	New York, N. Y.
Italian Apostolate Archdiocese of New York	1970	New York, N. Y.
Italian Board of Guardians	1936	Brooklyn, N. Y.
Italian Charities of America	1936	Elmhurst, N. Y.

Business and Civic	Founded	Location
Italian Cloak Suit & Skirt Makers Union - Local 48 - International Ladies Garment Workers' Union	1916	New York, N. Y.
Italian Dress & Waistmakers' Union - Local 89 - International Ladies Garment Workers' Union	1919	New York, N. Y.
Italian Seaman's Club	1970	New York, N. Y.
Italian Welfare League	1920	New York, N. Y.
Italo-American Professional Women, Inc.	1950	Brooklyn, N. Y.
Italy-America Chamber of Commerce	1887	New York, N. Y.
National Italian American League to Combat Defamation, Inc.	1958	New York, N. Y.
Orphans of Italy	1950	Upper Montclair, N. J.
UNICO National	1922	St. Louis, Mo.
United Italian American Labor Council	1941	New York, N. Y.
United Italian American League	1950	New York, N. Y.

Cultural, Fraternal and Social	Founded	Location
America Italy Society	1949	New York, N. Y.
Italian Actors Union	1920's	New York, N. Y.
Italian Cultural Center, Inc.	1965	L. I. C., N. Y.
Italian Cultural Institute	1957	New York, N. Y.
Italo-American National Union	1895	Chicago, Ill.
Sons of Italy Supreme Lodge		Phila., Penna.
Tiro a Segno of New York, Inc.	1889	New York, N. Y.

Historical and Educational	Founded	Location
American Association of Teachers of Italian	1924	Spokane, Washington
American Italian Congress	1949	Brooklyn, N. Y.
American Italian Historical Association	1966	Staten Island, N. Y.
Casa Italiana (Columbia University	1927	New York, N. Y.
Center for Migration Studies, Inc.	1965	Staten Island, N. Y.
Columbia Association of the Board of Education	1950	Queens, N. Y.
Italian Historical Society of America	1949	Brooklyn, N. Y.

Religious	Founded	Location
American Federation of Italian Evangelicals		Phila., Pa.
Italian Baptist Association of America	1898	Phila., Pa.
Italian Catholic Federation Central Council	1924	San Francisco, Calif.
St. Gennaro Society	1927	New York, N. Y.

Italian-American ethnic literature has developed only in the last fifty years, and its contributions are numerically few. Nonetheless, some powerful themes emerged among these writers. The subjects ranged from the gut problems of the early immigrant through periods of nostalgia for the old country at one time, rejection of it at another time and finally to the theme of "belonging to" the American scene.

AUTHOR	TITLE
ANGELO, Valenti	The Golden Gate. (1939)
	The Hill of Little Miracles. (1942)
	The Rooster Club. (1944)
	Bells of Bleeker Street. (1949)
BASSO, Hamilton	Days Before Lent. (1939)
	The View from Pompey's Head. (1954)
BENASUTTI, Marion	No Steady Job for Papa. (1966)
CALITRI, Charles	Strike Heaven in the Face. (1958)
CANIZIO, Frank.	A Man Against Fate. (1958)
CANZONERI, Robert	I Do So Politely. (1965)
	Men With Little Hammers. (1969)
CARUSO, Joseph	The Priest. (1956)
CAUTELA, Giuseppe	Moon Harvest. (1925)
CENEDELLA, Robert	A Little to the East. (1963)
CREATORE, Luigi	This World is Mine. (1942)

D'AGOSTINO, Guido   Olives on the Apple Tree.   (1940)

                                    Hills Beyond Manhattan.   (1942)

                                    My Enemy, The World.   (1947)

DE CAPITE, Michael   Maria.   (1943)

                                    No Bright Banner.   (1944)

                                    The Bennett Place.   (1948)

DE CAPITE, Raymond   The Coming of Fabrizze.   (1960)

                                    A Lost King.   (1961)

DE VOTO, Bernard   Rain Before Seven.   (1940)

DI DONATO, Pietro   Christ in Concrete.   (1939)

                                    Three Circles of Light.   (1960)

FANTE, Giovanni   Wait Until Spring, Bandini.   (1938)

                                    Ask the Dust.   (1939)

                                    Dago Red.   (1940)

FORGIONE, Louis   Men of Silence.   (1928)

                                      The River Between.   (1928)

FUMENTO, Rocco   Tree of Dark Reflection.   (1962)

GALLICO, Paul   The Small Miracle.   (1952)

LAMPEDUSA, Giuseppe di   The Leopard (1958)

LAPOLLA, Garibaldi Marto   The Grand Gennaro.   (1935)

LONGO, Lucas   The Family on Vendetta Street.   (1968)

MANGIONE, Jerre   Mount Allegro. (1942)

           Reunion in Sicily. (1950)

           Night Search. (1965)

MARZANI, Carl   The Survivor. (1958)

MOROSO, John Antonio The Stumbling Herd. (1923)

PAGANO, Joe   Golden Wedding. (1943)

           The Paesanos. (1940)

           The Condemned. (1947)

PANETTA, George   We Ride a White Donkey. (1944)

           Jimmy Potts Gets a Haircut, (1947)

PASINETTI, P.M.   Venetian Red. (1960)

           The Smile on the Face of the Lion.
                 (1965)

PETRACCA, Joseph   Come Back to Sorrento. (1948)

POLLINI, Francis   Glover. (1965)

PUZO, Mario   Dark Arena. (1953)

           The Fortunate Pilgrim. (1965)

           The Godfather. (1969)

SAVO, Jimmy   Little World, "Hello." (1947)

TALESE, Gay   The Bridge. (1964)

           Honor Thy Father. (1971)

TOMASI, Mari   Deep Grow the Roots. (1940)

                                Like Lesser Gods. (1949)

TUCCI, Niccolo   Before My Time. (1962)

VENTURA, Luigi Donato   Peppino. (1913)

VILLA, Silvio   Claudio Graziani. (1919)

VERGARA, Joe   Love and Pasta. (1969)

WINWAR, Frances   Gallows Hill. (1937)

    The following are critiques and analyses of the Italian-American
Novel:

PERAGALLO, Olga   Italian-American Authors and Their
                                Contribution to American Literature.
                                (1949)

GREEN, Rose Basile   The Evolution of Italian-American
                                Fiction as a Document of the Interaction
                                of Two Cultures. (ph.D. dissertation,
                                University of Pennsylvania, 1962)

SWEET, Mary M   The Italian Immigrant and His Reading.
                                (1925)

PAINTERS AND SCULPTORS

Those fields of art - painting, sculpture, frescoes and the like, are the natural home grounds of the Italians; most of them in the great classical tradition of Italy. Italian - Americans have also made contributions.

ABBATE, S. Paolo — Curator of Torrington Museum in Torrington, Connecticut. His works include two Dante monuments in Newburgh, New York, and Providence, Rhode Island.

BOROTTO, Enrico — Arrived in New York in 1925. Well-known wood-carver; specialization: wood-carving, sacred statues, altars and picture frames for ecclesiastical purposes.

CIAMPAGLIA, Carlo — Mural painter; decorated Court House, Sunbury, Pennsylvania, Fairmont Mausoleum, Newark, New Jersey; designed murals of Food Building, New York World's Fair, 1939.

D'ANDREA, Albert Philip — Artist, born in Italy. Portraits includes: Bernard M. Baruch, 1954; Dr. W.B. Guthrie, 1939; and Dean E. R. Mosher. His works in the collections of the Library of Congress and Smithsonian Institute, Washington, D.C.

FRANZONI, Carlo — "Car of History", in 1816, in Statuary Hall, Washington, D. C.

GREGORI, Luigi — Affiliated with Notre Dame University for 17 years, beginning about 1874. His works adorn the Golden Dome of Notre Dame University and the walls of the University's administration building.

LAZZARI, Pietro — Sculptor - Painter, born in Italy. Executed busts of Eleanor Roosevelt, Norman Thomas, Adlai Stevenson and Pope Paul VI. Developer of polychrome concrete. Works exhibited and represented in a number of museums - including the Smithsonian Institute, Washington, D.C. and the San Francisco Museum, California.

MANGRAVITE, Peppino

Painter, born 1896; Chairman of the Department of Painting and Sculpture at Columbia University, New York, from 1956 to 1964. His works have been exhibited nationally and internationally. Mosaic murals, in St. Anthony's Shrine, Boston, Massachusetts and the United States Post Office Building, Hempstead, New York.

MARTINELLI, Ezio

Sculptor, born 1913, New Jersey. Works are in the permanent collections of Whitney Museum, New York, Brooks Memorial, Memphis, Tennessee; Guggenheim Museum, New York City, the Newark Museum, New Jersey, and in the General Assembly building of the United Nations, New York City.

PICCIRILLI, Attilio (and his five artist brothers)

Monuments to Battleship Maine and Firemen's Memorial in New York; carved the statue of Lincoln in the Lincoln Memorial in Washington, D. C., from the plastic model by the illustrious Daniel Chester French.

RUSSO, Gaetano

Columbus Monument in Columbus Circle, New York.

STELLA, Frank

Painter, born in Massachusetts. Among his many works are: "The Marriage of Reason and Squalor", 1959, (in the collection of the Museum of Modern Art, New York City); and "Telluride", 1960, (in Carter Burden's collection, New York.)

STELLA, Joseph

Painter, born in Italy. His many works include: "Battle of Light Coney Island" (1913), and "Brooklyn Bridge" (1917), in the Yale University Art Gallery, New Haven, Connecticut. Among his many works in the collection of the Museum of Modern Art, New York City, are: "Factories" (1918) and "Song of the Nightingale" (1918).

VITTOR, Frank

Columbus Statue in Schenley Park, Pittsburgh, Pennsylvania.

ALBERGHETTI, Anna Maria	Actress, singer, recording artist.
ALDA, Alan	Stage, screen and television actor.
ALDA, Robert	Stage, screen and television actor.
AMECHE, Don	Screen actor. Portrayed Alexander Graham Bell.
ANSARA, Michael	Screen and television actor.
ARIA, Pietro	Born in Italy. Composed the biblical opera JERICHO ROAD and dedicated it to Pope Paul in 1966.
ARDEN, Toni	Popular singer and recording artist.
BANCROFT, Anne (nee Italiano, Anna Maria)	Born in New York City. Famous stage and screen actress. 1962 Academy Award winner as the Best Actress for her role in the Miracle Worker.
BENNETT, Tony (nee Benedetto)	Born in New York City. Popular television star and recording artist. Recipient of 1967 Gold Record Award for the album TONY BENNETT'S GREATEST HITS, Volume 3.
BERARDINELLI, Nicola	Conductor and composer for four different opera companies. Composed AVE MARIA and MY ROSARY.
BIFERI, Nicolas	In 1774 established a music and dance school for young ladies; possibly the first of its kind on this continent. Was a noted Neapolitan harpsichordist and gave recitals in New York.
BONO, Sonny	. . . .of the Sonny & Cher team. Popular entertainers and recording artists. Recipient of 1965 Gold Record Award for I GOT YOU, BABE, and LOOK AT US.
BORGNINE, Ernest	Born in Hamden, Connecticut; stage and screen actor. 1955 Academy Award winner for his role in Marty.

BRAZZI, Rossano

Actor. Starred in the film version of South Pacific.

BUZZI, Ruth

Born in Westerly, Rhode Island; popular comedienne.

CAPRA, Frank

Famous Hollywood movie director. Academy Award winner as Best Director in: 1934 for It Happened One Night 1936 for Mr. Deeds Goes to Town, and 1938 for You Can't Take It With You.

CARRADINE, John

Born in New York City. Star of stage and screen; best known as a Shakespearean actor.

COCO, James

Born in New York City; stage and screen actor. Appeared in Last of the Red Hot Lovers.

CONTE, Richard

Born in New York City; popular screen and television star.

COOPER, Pat

Popular comedian and recording star.

COSTELLO, Lou

Born in Paterson, New Jersey; comedian; of the famous Abbott and Costello comedy team.

DALLAPICCOLA, Luigi

Italian born composer, pianist and music teacher. Occupied the Chair of Italian Culture at the University of California.

DAMONE, Vic
(nee Vito Farinola)

Born in New York City; popular singer, entertainer and recording artist.

DARIN, Bobby

Born in New York City; popular singer screen and television star, and composer of popular music. Recipient of the 1959 Grammy Awards for Best New Artist and Best Song, MACK THE KNIFE.

DE LUISE, Dom

Born in Brooklyn, New York. Popular comedian and television star.

DUSE, Eleanora

Came to America from Italy in 1893; was one of the great actresses of her day. Her Camille brought more money at the box office than Sarah Bernhardt's Camille. President Cleveland gave a reception at the White House in her honor.

DRAKE, Alfred

Born in New York City; popular and well known singer of stage, radio, screen and recording star. Starred in the Broadway plays: Oklahoma, Carousel, Kiss Me Kate.

FRANCIOSA, Anthony

Born in New York City. Popular television and screen actor.

FRANCHI, Sergio

Popular singer, television and screen star.

FRANCIS, Connie

Born in Newark, New Jersey; popular singer and recording artist.

FUNICELLO, Annette

Born in Utica, New York; television star; one of the original stars of Walt Disney's Mousketeers.

GATTI-CASAZZA, Giulio

Operatic manager for the Metropolitan Opera House from 1908 to 1934.

GAZZARA, Ben

Born in New York City; actor, director and producer.

GENNARO, Peter

Born in Metairie, Louisiana; famous stage and television choreographer.

GARAGIOLA, Joe

Born in St. Louis, Missouri; television emcee; former baseball player.

GRECO, Jose

Born in Italy; famous flamenco dancer.

GRECO, Buddy

Born in Philadelphia, Pennsylvania; popular entertainer, singer and recording artist.

GUARDINO, Harry

Born in New York City; popular television, stage and screen star.

JAMES, Dennis — Born in Jersey City, New Jersey; television Emcee.

JAMES, Joni — Born in Chicago, Illinois; popular singer and recording artist.

JOIO, Norman Dello — 1957 Pulitzer Prize Award for his musical composition of: MEDITATIONS ON ECCLESIASTES.

KING, Morgana — Stylist and actress.

LAINE, Frankie — Popular singer and recording artist.

LAWRENCE, Carol — Born in Melrose Park, Illinois; stage, television actress, singer and dancer.

LA ROSA, Julius — Television entertainer and recording artist; now a radio disc jockey.

LISI, Virna — Italian born actress; Hollywood star.

LOLLOBRIGIDA, Gina — Italian born actress; Hollywood star.

LOMBARDO, Guy — Born in London, Canada; popular orchestra leader.

LOREN, Sophia — Italian born actress. 1961 Academy Award Winner as Best Actress for her role in Two Women.

MANCINI, Henry — Born in Cleveland, Ohio; composer, arranger and director. 1962 Academy Award winner for his musical composition of MOON RIVER and recipient of many Grammy Awards. 1963 Academy Award winner for his musical composition of DAYS OF WINE & ROSES.

MANTOVANI, Annunzio — Orchestra leader and recording artist. Recipient of the 1961 Gold Record Awards for CHRISTMAS CAROLS, THEATRE LAND FILM ENCORES, Volume 1 and GEMS FOREVER, etc.

MARTIN, Dean (ne´ (Dino Crocetti)	Born in Steubenville, Ohio; popular television and screen star; singer and recording artist. Received many Gold Record Awards.
MASTROIANNI, Marcello	Italian born actor; Hollywood star.
MINELLI, Liza	Born in Los Angeles, California; daughter of Judy Garland and Vincente Minelli. Famous and popular star of television screen, stage and recording artist.
MINELLI, Vincente	Born in Chicago, Illinois; movie director. 1958 Academy Award winner for the musical film Gigi, which film won nine Oscars that year.
MONICA, Corbett	Entertainer and comedian.
PIAZZA, Ben	Born in Little Rock, Arkansas; stage actor. Won Theatre World Award for Kataki. Has appeared in both motion pictures and television; and also wrote a novel and several plays.
PINZA, Ezio	Italian born basso, made his debut at the Metropolitan Opera House in 1926. Created a sensation in the stage versions of South Pacific and Fanny.
PISTON, Walter	Professor Emeritus of Music at Harvard University. 1948 Pulitzer Prize Winner for his SYMPHONY NUMBER THREE.
PRIMA, Louis	Popular entertainer, orchestra leader and recording artist.
RICCI, Ruggiero	American violinist.
SCALA, Gia	Born in Liverpool, England; actress; appeared in The Guns Of Navarone and Don't Go Near The Water.

SECONDARI, John

Television producer, narrator; and authored <u>Coins In The Fountain</u> in 1954 and <u>Temptation For A King</u> in 1954 and <u>Spinner Of The Dream</u> in 1955.

SINATRA, Frank Jr.

Born in Jersey City, New Jersey; popular singer; son of Frank Sinatra.

SINATRA, Nancy

Born in Jersey City, New Jersey; popular singer and recording artist; daughter of Frank Sinatra. Received the Gold Record Award in 1966 for THESE BOOTS ARE MADE FOR WALKIN'.

STUART, Enzo

Tenor; popular recording artist. Racing car enthusiast.

TRAGETTA, Philip

Musician and composer; friend of Presidents James Madison and James Monroe. Established American Conservatory in Philadelphia.

VACCARO, Brenda

Born in Brooklyn, New York; popular stage and television star.

VALE, Jerry

Born in New York City; popular singer of Italian folk songs.

VALENTE, Caterina

Born in Paris, France; world famous singer, dancer and musician; popular television star and recording artist.

VALERIANI, Richard

NBC television news reporter.

ZEFFERELLI, Franco

Born in Florence, Italy. Theatrical and operatic director - designer. Currently at the Metropolitan Opera House.

METROPOLITAN OPERA HOUSE

SINGERS

The stage of the Metropolitan Opera House glittered with the brilliance of the most famous and glamorous stars of the opera world. From its inception in 1883 to its sad demise in 1966, approximately 1,600 stars sang and appeared there. Of this number not less than 354 were Italian. The list below is merely representative of those Italians and Italian-Americans who most endeared themselves to the music loving public.

NAME	VOICE RANGE	DATE OF DEBUT
ALBANESE, Licia	Soprano	February 9, 1940
AMARA, Lucine	Soprano	November 6, 1950
AMATO, Pasquale	Baritone	November 20, 1908
ANCONA, Mario	Baritone	December 11, 1893
BACCALONI, Salvatore	Bass	December 7, 1940
BARDELLI, Cesare	Baritone	April 6, 1957
BERGONZI, Carlo	Tenor	November 13, 1956
BONELLI, Richard	Baritone	December 1, 1932
BORI, Lucrezia	Soprano	November 11, 1912
CARUSO, Enrico	Tenor	November 23, 1903
COLOMBATI, Virginia	Soprano	December 11, 1893
CORELLI, Franco	Tenor	January 27, 1961
CORENA, Fernando	Bass	February 6, 1954
COSTA, Mary	Soprano	January 6, 1964
DELLA CASA, Lisa	Soprano	November 20, 1953
DEL MONACO, Mario	Tenor	November 27, 1950
DEL LUCA, Giuseppe	Baritone	November 25, 1915

NAME	VOICE RANGE	DATE OF DEBUT
DI STEFANO, Giuseppe	Tenor	February 25, 1948
FERNANDI, Eugenio	Tenor	February 19, 1958
GALLI-CURCI, Amelita	Soprano	November 14, 1921
GIGLI, Beniamino	Tenor	November 26, 1920
GOBBI, Tito	Baritone	January 13, 1956
MARTINELLI, Giovanni	Tenor	November 20, 1913
MELBA, Nellie	Soprano	December 4, 1893
MOFFO, Anna	Soprano	November 14, 1959
MORELLI, Carlo	Baritone	December 21, 1935
MOSCONA, Nicolo	Bass	December 13, 1937
PATTI, Adelina	Soprano	April 2, 1892
PIAZZA, Marguerite	Soprano	January 4, 1951
PINZA, Ezio	Bass	November 1, 1926
PONSELLE, Carmela	Mezzo	December 5, 1925
PONSELLE, Rosa	Soprano	November 15, 1918
SCHIPA, Tito	Tenor	November 23, 1932
SCOTTO, Renata	Soprano	October 13, 1965
SERENI, Mario	Baritone	November 9, 1957
SIEPI, Cesare	Bass	November 6, 1950
TAGLIAVINI, Ferruccio	Tenor	January 10, 1947
TAJO, Italo	Bass	December 28, 1948
TAMAGNO, Francesco	Tenor	November 21, 1894
TEBALDI, Renata	Soprano	January 31, 1955

NAME	VOICE RANGE	DATE OF DEBUT
TETRAZZINI, Luisa	Soprano	December 27, 1911
TOZZI, Giorgio	Bass	March 9, 1955
TUCCI, Gabriella	Soprano	October 29, 1960
VALDENGO, Giuseppe	Baritone	December 19, 1947
VALENTINO, Frank	Baritone	December 9, 1940

METROPOLITAN OPERA HOUSE

CONDUCTORS

The list of conductors is also an impressive "Who's Who". Throughout its 83 years of existence the Metropolitan Opera House was host to no less than 101 conductors, of whom 34 were Italian.
The more popularly known among the Italians were:

NAME	DATE OF DEBUT
ANTONICELLI, Giuseppe	November 10, 1947
ARDITI, Luigi	April 2, 1892
BARBINI, Ernesto	March 4, 1952
BAVAGNOLI, Gaetano	November 19, 1915
BELLEZZA, Vincenzo	November 4, 1926
BEVIGNANI, Enrico	November 29, 1893
CALUSIO, Ferruccio	December 12, 1940
CAMPANINI, Cleofonte	November 3, 1883
CELLINI, Renato	April 9, 1952
CIMARA, Pietro	March 11, 1932
CLEVA, Fausto	February 14, 1942
EREDE, Alberto	November 11, 1950
FERRARI, Rodolfo	November 18, 1907
GARDELLI, Lamberto	January 30, 1966
LA MARCHINA, Robert	December 31, 1964
MONTEMEZZI, Italo	February 7, 1941
MORANZONI, Roberto	November 12, 1917
PANIZZA, Ettore	December 22, 1934
PAPI, Gennaro	November 16, 1916

NAME	DATE OF DEBUT
PODESTI, Vittorio	November 18, 1909
POLACCO, Giorgio	November 11, 1912
SANTI, Nello	January 25, 1962
SEPPILLI, Armando	December 7, 1895
SETTI, Giulio	February 12, 1922
SODERO, Cesare	November 28, 1942
SOLTI, Georg	December 17, 1960
SPETRINO, Francesco	November 20, 1908
STURANI, Giuseppe	November 22, 1911
TANGO, Egisto	November 22, 1909
TOSCANINI, Arturo	November 16, 1908
TRUCCO, Victor	March 2, 1962
VERCHI, Nino	October 31, 1959
VIANESI, Auguste	October 22, 1883
VIGNA, Arturo	November 23, 1903

ITALIAN AMERICANS IN THE UNITED STATES CONGRESS

Ninety-Second Congress (July, 1971)

HOUSE OF REPRESENTATIVES

NAME	STATE	DISTRICT	PARTY
LEGGETT, Robert	California	4	(D)
MILLER, George	California	8	(D)
GIAIMO, Robert N.	Connecticut	3	(D)
GRASSO, Ella T.	Connecticut	6	(D)
FASCELL, Dante	Florida	12	(D)
ANNUNZIO, Frank	Illinois	7	(D)
MAZZOLI, Romano L.	Kentucky	3	(D)
CONTE, Silvio O.	Massachusetts	1	(R)
MINISH, Joseph	New Jersey	11	(D)
RODINO, Peter W., Jr.	New Jersey	10	(D)
ADDABBO, Joseph P.	New York	7	(D)
BRASCO, Frank J.	New York	11	(D)
BIAGGI, Mario	New York	24	(D)
LATTA, Delbert L.	Ohio	5	(R)
MURPHY, John M.	New York	16	(D)
VIGORITO, Joseph P.	Pennsylvania	24	(D)
RONCALIO, Teno	Wyoming	At Large	(D)

THE SENATE

NAME	STATE	DISTRICT	PARTY
PASTORE, John O.	Rhode Island	----	(D)

ITALIAN-AMERICANS IN THE FEDERAL AND STATE JUDICIARY

The number of judges of Italian origin is impressive. In 1965 there was organized the American Justinian Society of Jurists consisting of judges of Italian origin. This society reports that there are over 675 judges in the United States of Italian heritage.

FEDERAL COURTS

HON. RUGGERO J. ALDISERT	Circuit Judge, Third Circuit
HON. ANTHONY T. AUGELLI	District Judge, District of New Jersey
HON. FRANK J. BATTISTI	District Judge, Northern District of Ohio
HON. JOHN G. CANNELLA	District Judge, Southern District of New York
HON. ANTHONY J. CELEBREZZE	Circuit Judge, Fifth Circuit
HON. MARK A. COSTANTINO	District Judge, Eastern District of New York
HON. LEE P. GAGLIARDI	District Judge, Southern District of New York
HON. EDMUND L. PALMIERI	District Judge, Southern District of New York
HON. RAYMOND J. PETTINE	District Judge, District Court of Rhode Island
HON. PAUL P. RAO	Judge, U. S. Customs Court
HON. EDWARD D. RE	Judge, U. S. Customs Court
HON. JOHN J. SIRICA	District Judge, District Court of the District Columbia
HON. ANTHONY J. TRAVIA	District Judge, Eastern District of New York
HON. ROBERT C. ZAMPANO	District Judge, District Court of Connecticut

HON. ALFONSO J. ZIRPOLI   District Judge,
                                 Northern District of California

HIGHEST STATE COURTS

JUDGE JOHN F. SCILEPPI   New York

CHIEF JUSTICE G. JOSEPH TAURÒ   Massachusetts

JUSTICE FRANCIS J. QUIRICO   Massachusetts

JUSTICE THOMAS J. PAOLINO   Rhode Island

ITALIAN AMERICANS IN FEDERAL DEPARTMENTS AND AGENCIES OF THE UNITED STATES GOVERNMENT

(Heads of Departments - 1971)

Name	Position	Department/Agency
CAMPIOLI, Mario E.	Acting Architect of Capitol	Architect of the Capitol
SICILIANO, Rocco C.	Undersecretary of Commerce	Department of Commerce
PODESTA, Robert A.	Assistant Secretary of Commerce for Economic Development	Department of Commerce
PELLERZI, Leo M.	Assistant Attorney General for Administration	Department of Justice
DE PALMA, Samuel	Assistant Secretary for International Organization Affairs	Department of State
VOLPE, John A.	Secretary of Transportation	Department of Transportation

STATE ASSEMBLYMEN AND REPRESENTATIVES

Italian-American Senators and Assemblymen or Representatives in the 1971 legislatures of the states of California, Connecticut, Illinois, Pennsylvania, Massachusetts, New Jersey and New York; chosen because of the great number of Italian ethnics in those jurisdictions.

STATE OF CALIFORNIA

SENATE

GREGORIO, Arlen	(D)
LAGOMARSINO, Robert J.	(R)
MOSCONE, George R.	(D)

ASSEMBLY

BAGLEY, William T.	(R)
BELOTTI, Frank P.	(R)
CHAPPIE, Eugene	(R)
MORETTI, Bob	(D)
PRIOLO, Paul	(R)
ROBERTI, David A.	(D)

Source: The Book of the States. Supplement to the Directory of State Legislators, 1971.

STATE OF CONNECTICUT

SENATE

ALFANO, Charles	(D)	FAULISO, Joseph J.	(D)
CIARLONE, Anthony M.	(D)	MONDANI, Thomas P.	(D)
CUTILLO, Louis	(D)	PETRONI, Romeo G.	(R)
DE NARDIS, Lawrence J.	(R)	PRETE, John D.	(D)
DINELLI, Joseph J.	(D)	STRADA, William E., Jr.	(D)

HOUSE OF REPRESENTATIVES

AJELLO, Carl R.	(D)	DZIALO, Raymond J.	(D)
ARGAZZI, Robert A.	(R)	ESPOSITO, Donald F.	(D)
AVCOLLIE, Bernard	(D)	FABRIGIO, John A.	(R)
BADALATO, Dominic J.	(D)	FRATE, Gennaro W.	(R)
BOGGINI, N. Charles	(D)	GAGLIARDI, Vincent	(D)
BONETTI, Addo E.	(D)	GENOVESI, Donald S.	(R)
BRUNO, Robert G.	(R)	GIAMO, Thomas J.	(D)
CARROZELLA, John A.	(D)	GROPPO, John G.	(D)
CIAMPI, Francis W.	(D)	GUIDERA, George C.	(R)
COLUCCI, Michael R.	(D)	LA GROTTA, Guido	(R)
COSTELLO, Philip N., Jr.	(R)	LA ROSA, Paul	(D)
CRETELLA, Albert W., Jr.	(R)	MAIOCCO, John P., Jr.	(D)
DE BAISE, Pasquale J.	(D)	MASTRIANNI, Silvio A.	(D)
DELLA VECCHIA, Arthur	(D)	MESITE, Patsy J.	(D)
DI MEO, Lucien	(R)	MORANO, Michael L.	(R)
D'ONOFRIO, John	(D)	MOTTO, Nicholas M.	(D)

NIGRO, Sabath M.	(D)	PROVENZANO, Albert	(D)
PALMIERI, James J.	(D)	PUGLIESE, Joseph M.	(R)
PANUZIO, Nicholas A.	(R)	STROFFOLINO, Louis J.	(R)
PAOLETTA, Leonard S.	(R)	TACINELLI, Edward J.	(D)
PAPANDREA, John F.	(D)	TANESZIO, Theresa	(D)
PIAZZA, Louis J.	(D)	VICINO, Robert J.	(D)
POVINELLI, Henry A.	(R)	VOTTO, Louis S.	(D)

STATE OF ILLINOIS

SENATE

ROMANO, Sam   (D)

HOUSE OF REPRESENTATIVES

ARRIGO, Victor	(D)	GIORGI, E. J.	(D)
BARRY, Toby	(D)	GRANATA, Peter C.	(R)
CALVO, Horace L.	(D)	LAURINO, William J.	(D)
CAPPARELLI, Ralph C.	(D)	HANAHAN, Thomas	(D)
CAPUZI, Louis F.	(R)	MERLO, John	(D)
DI PRIMA, Lawrence	(D)	SCARIANO, Anthony	(D)

STATE OF MASSACHUSETTS

SENATE

CONTE, John J.	(D)	NUCIFORO, Andrea F.	(D)
DI CARLO, Joseph J. C.	(D)	PELLEGRINI, Philibert L.	(D)
FONSECA, Mary L.	(D)	UMANA, Mario	(D)

HOUSE OF REPRESENTATIVES

BELMONTE, Robert A.	(R)	LANGONE, Joseph A.	(D)
BERTONAZZI, Louis P.	(D)	LOMBARDI, Michael J.	(D)
BEVILACQUA, Francis J.	(D)	MATRANGO, Frank J.	(D)
BOVERINI, Walter J.	(D)	MORINI, Louis J.	(R)
BUFFONE, Charles J.	(D)	NICKINELLO, Louis R.	(D)
BUGLIONE, Nicholas J.	(D)	PICUCCI, Angelo	(D)
BUSSONE, Thomas	(R)	PIRO, Vincent J.	(D)
COLLARO, Andrew	(D)	PITARO, Mimie B., Msgr.	(D)
COLO, H. Thomas	(D)	SACCO, George L.	(D)
DEL GROSSO, Joseph	(D)	SCALLI, Anthony J.	(D)
DI FRUSCIA, Anthony R.	(D)	SCIBELLI, Anthony M.	(D)
GALOTTI, Edward F.	(D)	SCLAFANI, Pasquale	(D)
GRIMALDI, James L.	(D)	SEMENSI, Joseph J.	(D)
GROSSO, Anthony P.	(R)	SIRIANNI, Ralph E., Jr.	(D)
GUZZI, Paul H.	(D)		

STATE OF NEW JERSEY

SENATE

AZZOLINA, Joseph	(R)	MARESSA, Joseph A.	(D)
CAFIERO, James S.	(R)	MARAZITI, Joseph J.	(R)
GIULIANO, Michael A.	(R)	MERLINO, Joseph P.	(D)
DE ROSE, Ralph C.	(D)	MUSTO, William V.	(D)
ITALIANO, Frank C.	(R)	RINALDO, Matthew J.	(R)
LAZZARA, Joseph A.	(D)	SCHIAFFO, Alfred D.	(R)

GENERAL ASSEMBLY

BASSANO, C. Louis	(R)	IMPERIALE, Anthony	(I)
CHINNICI, Joseph	(R)	LE FANTE, Joseph A.	(D)
COLASURDO, James A.	(D)	MANCINI, James J.	(R)
DE KORTE, Richard W.	(R)	MENZA, Alexander J.	(D)
ESPOSITO, Michael P.	(D)	ORECHIO, Carl	(R)
FAILLA, Silvio	(D)	PARETI, Harold	(R)
FIORE, C. Richard	(R)	PELLECCHIA, Vincent O.	(D)
FLORIO, James J.	(D)	RUSSO, Peter J.	(R)
GARIBALDI, Peter P.	(R)	SPIZZIRI, John A.	(R)

STATE OF NEW YORK

SENATE

CALANDRA, John D.	(R)	LOMBARDI, Tarky J., Jr.	(R)
FERRARO, Nicholas	(D)	MARCHI, John J.	(R)
GIOFFRE, Anthony B.	(R)	MARINO, Ralph J.	(R)
GIUFFREDA, Leon F.	(R)	SANTUCCI, John J.	(D)

ASSEMBLY

BATTISTA, Vito P.	(R)	LISA, Joseph F.	(D)
BERSANI, Leonard F.	(R)	LO PRESTO, John G.	(R)
BIONDO, Peter R.	(R)	MARGIOTTA, Joseph M.	(D)
CALABRETTA, Joseph S.	(D)	MARTUSCELLO, Joseph M.	
CINCOTTA, George A.	(D)	MERCORELLA, Anthony J.	
DELLI BOVI, Alfred A.	(R)	MIRTO, Peter G.	(D)
DE SALVIO, Louis	(D)	MONDELLO, Ferdinand J.	(D)
DI CARLO, Dominick L.	(R)	PASSANNANTE, William F.	
DI FALCO, Anthony G.	(D)	PISANI, Joseph R.	(R)
GIORDANO, William J.	(D)	RICCIO, Vincent	(R)
GRECO, Stephen R.	(D)	ROSSETTI, Frank G.	(D)
GRIECO, Salvatore J.	(D)	RUSSO, Lucio F.	(R)
LAMA, Alfred A.	(D)	STELLA, Anthony J.	(D)

STATE OF PENNSYLVANIA

SENATE

CIANFRANI, Henry J.	(D)	MELLOW, Robert J.	(D)
MAZZEI, Frank	(D)	ZEMPRELLI, Edward P.	(D)

HOUSE OF REPRESENTATIVES

BELLOMINI, Robert	(D)	LAUDADIO, John F., Sr.	(D)
BONETTO, Joseph F.	(D)	MANDERINO, James	(D)
BUTERA, Robert J.	(R)	MARTINO, Leonard L.	(D)
CAPUTO, Charles N.	(D)	MASTRANGELO, Adriano	(R)
COPPOLINO, Matthew F.	(R)	MUSTO, Raphael A.	(D)
DE MEDIO, A. J.	(D)	RUGGIERO, Philip	(D)
DININNI, Rudolph	(R)	SCIRICA, Anthony J.	(R)
KELLY PALERMO, Anita	(D)	VALICENTI, A. Joseph	(D)

STATISTICS

ITALIANS WHO REPORTED UNDER THE ALIEN
ADDRESS PROGRAM
AND STATES OF RESIDENCE DURING 1970

State of Residence	Number
Alabama	82
Alaska	12
Arizona	200
Arkansas	51
California	13,772
Colorado	597
Connecticut	15,192
Delaware	402
District of Columbia	365
Florida	1,460
Georgia	138
Hawaii	45
Idaho	46
Illinois	16,175
Indiana	442
Iowa	194
Kansas	105
Kentucky	125
Louisiana	730

State of Residence	Number
Maine	162
Maryland	2,668
Massachusetts	16,024
Michigan	7,678
Minnesota	166
Mississippi	78
Missouri	1,552
Montana	57
Nebraska	158
Nevada	177
New Hampshire	110
New Jersey	28,932
New Mexico	88
New York	94,962
North Carolina	142
North Dakota	14
Ohio	7,371
Oklahoma	76
Oregon	255
Pennsylvania	17,261
Rhode Island	2,865
South Carolina	81
South Dakota	10

State of Residence	Number
Tennessee	125
Texas	703
Utah	168
Vermont	128
Virginia	529
Washington	857
West Virginia	643
Wisconsin	1,499
Wyoming	32

U. S. Territories & Possessions:

Guam	7
Puerto Rico	121
Virgin Islands	10

TOTAL: 235,842

* Source: 1970 Annual Report, Immigration & Naturalization Service, Washington, D. C.

STATISTICS

ITALIAN IMMIGRANTS ADMITTED AND STATE OF INTENDED PERMANENT RESIDENCE: YEAR ENDED JUNE 30, 1970.

State of intended permanent residence	Number
Alabama	16
Alaska	1
Arizona	17
Arkansas	9
California	910
Colorado	49
Connecticut	1,812
Delaware	63
District of Columbia	30
Florida	121
Georgia	16
Hawaii	5
Idaho	8
Illinois	1,873
Indiana	53
Iowa	19
Kansas	7
Kentucky	24
Louisiana	23

State of intended permanent residence	Number
Maine	16
Maryland	160
Massachusetts	1,709
Michigan	822
Minnesota	29
Mississippi	6
Missouri	110
Montana	2
Nebraska	13
Nevada	10
New Hampshire	17
New Jersey	3,378
New Mexico	7
New York	10,809
North Carolina	19
North Dakota	-
Ohio	630
Oklahoma	17
Oregon	9
Pennsylvania	1,376
Rhode Island	396
South Carolina	11
South Dakota	2

State of intended permanent residence	Number
Tennessee	4
Texas	59
Utah	11
Vermont	19
Virginia	60
Washington	33
West Virginia	34
Wisconsin	131
Wyoming	2

U. S. Territories and Possessions:

Guam	1
Puerto Rico	9
Virgin Islands	4
All other	2

TOTAL: 24,973

*Source: 1970 Annual Report, Immigration & Naturalization Service, Washington, D. C.

The name "COLUMBUS" is honored geographically in not less than thirty-five of our United States:

Alabama - Columbia, Houston County
Columbiana, Shelby County
Columbus City, Marshall County
Arkansas - Columbia County
California - Columbia, Tuoulmne County
Connecticut - Columbia, Tolland County
District of Columbia - Washington
Florida - Columbia County
Columbia, Columbia County
Georgia - Columbia County,
Columbus, Muscogee County
Illinois - Columbia, Monroe County
Columbus, Adams County
Indiana - Columbia City, Whitley County
Columbus, Bartholomew County
East Columbus, Bartholomew County
Iowa - Columbia, Marion County
Columbus City, Louisa County
Columbus Junction, Louisa County
Kansas - Columbus, Cherokee County
Kentucky - Columbia, Adair County
Columbus, Hickman County
Louisiana - Columbia, Caldwell County
Columbus, Sabine County
Maine - Columbia, Washington County
Columbia Falls, Washington County
Michigan - Columbiaville, Lapeer County
Minnesota - Columbia Heights, Anoka County
Mississippi - Columbia, Marion County
Columbia, Lowndes County
Missouri - Columbia, Boone County
Columbus, Johnson County
Montana - Columbia Falls, Flathead County
Columbus, Stillwater County
Nebraska - Columbus, Platte County
New Jersey - Columbia, Warren County
Columbus, Burlington County
New Mexico - Columbus, Luna County
New York - Columbia County
North Carolina - Columbus County
Columbia, Tyrrell County
Columbus, Polk County
North Dakota - Columbus, Burke County

114

Ohio - Columbiana County
    Columbia Station, Lorain County
    Columbiana, Columbiana County
    Columbus, Franklin County
Oregon - Columbia County
    Columbia City, Columbia County
Pennsylvania - Columbia County
    Columbia, Lancaster County
    Columbus, Warren County
South Carolina - Columbia, Richland County
    W. Columbia, Lexington County
South Dakota - Columbia, Brown County
Tennessee - Columbia, Maury County
Texas - Columbus, Colorado County
Utah - Columbia, Carbon County
Virginia - Columbia, Fluvanna County
    Columbia Furnance, Shenandoah County
Washington - Columbia County
Wisconsin - Columbia County
    Columbus, Columbia County

EDUCATORS

Education has been the heritage of Italy. A few of the Italian educators in the United States are:

CALABRESE, Giuseppe

Professor of Electrical Engineering at New York University in 1948; Assistant Engineer at Consolidated Edison Company from 1928 to 1948.

CALABRESE, Joseph V.

Founded school for exceptional children; President and Director of National Association for Retarded Children, former member of Colorado legislature.

CAPONIGRI, Aloysius Robert

Faculty member of Notre Dame University since 1946 and professor of philosophy at the same university since 1956. Author: History of Western Philosophy, (4 vols.), 1964; Masterpieces of Catholic Literature, (2 vols.), 1964, etc.

CORDASCO, Francesco

Professor of Educational Sociology at Montclair State College, New Jersey. Wrote many articles for magazines and introductions to a number of books. Authored (with S. La Gumina): Italians in the United States, 1971.

COSENZA, Mario

President of Brooklyn College, Brooklyn, New York, from 1938 to 1939. Recipient of the Certificate of Merit, Token Gratitude, 1960. Author: The Study of Italians in the United States, 1924; The Four Voyages of Amerigo Vespucci, 1907.

COVELLO, Leonard

Worked among the Italian immigrants and helped bring the Italian language into the high schools. Principal of Benjamin Franklin High School, Bronx, New York, from 1944 to 1948. Author: The Heart Is the Teacher, 1958.

DEFERRARI, Roy Joseph

Taught Latin and Greek at Princeton University, New Jersey, and Catholic University, Washington, D. C.

116

Author: Latin English Dictionary of
St. Thomas, 1960;
Complete Index of Summa Theologica of
St. Thomas, 1956;
Lexicon, Latin English of St. Thomas
Aquinas, 1953.

FRATTI, Mario

Professor of Romance Languages at
Hunter College, New York.
Author: Che, La Vittimia, Le Donne, and
La Mafia.

LEPIS, Louis

Educator, athlete.   Won many awards in
the athletic field; contributed numerous
writings in the field of public recreation.
Author: An Italian Named Smith (to be
published.)

LURAGHI, Raimondi

Professor of American History at the
University of Genoa, Italy. Lectured and
did research in American History at the
University of Richmond, Virginia.   His
book on the American Civil War contains
more than 1300 pages.

MARRARO, Dr. Howard

Former Professor of Italian at Columbia
University, New York.   Author of many
books on Italian literature, history, cul-
ture and relations with the United States.
Among his numerous articles are:
"Italo-Americans in Pennsylvania in the
18th Century", 1940; "Lincoln's Italian
Volunteers from New York", 1943.

MARTINETTI, Odino

President of Johnson Vermont Teachers
College, 1957.

MORTOLA, Edward J.

President of Pace College, New York,
from 1960 to date.   Author (with Lynn
H. Draper): Human Relations Pitfalls
for the Novice Administrators, 1953.

ORSINI, Gian Napoleone
        Giordano

Professor of English Literature; recip-
ient of: Guggenheim Grant, 1964 - 1965;
Senior Award National Foundation for
Arts and Humanities, 1967 - 1968.
Author of books on Tennyson, Milton,
Bacon, Macchiavelli, written in Italian.

PEI, Mario Andrew

Philologist, as well as an educator. Professor Emeritus of Romance Philology at Columbia University, New York. Author of numerous books. A few of his recent publications are: Words in Sheep's Clothing, 1969; The America we Lost, 1968; and What's in a Word, 1968.

PREZZOLINI, Giuseppe

Professor Emeritus of Italian at Columbia University, New York. He is an author and journalist, now residing in Switzerland and still comments on the Italian scene. He is also Director Emeritus of Casa Italiana, New York, New York.

ROSSINI, Dr. Frederick

Chemist as well as an educator. Appointed Dean of the Graduate School of the University of Notre Dame in 1960. Recipient of the Gold Medal Award from the Department of Commerce, 1950; Laetare Medal from the University of Notre Dame, 1965, and several other awards.

RICCIO, Peter

Director Emeritus of Casa Italiana and Professor Emeritus of Italian at Columbia University, New York. Professor Riccio was one of the founders of the Casa Italiana.

SALVADORI, Mario G.

Professor of civil engineering and architecture at Columbia University, New York, from 1940 to the present. Author (with M. P. Levy): Mathematics in Architecture, 1968; Structural Design in Architecture, 1967, etc.

SALVEMINI, Gaetano

Historian as well as an educator. His history of the French Revolution and his work on Giuseppe Mazzini are regarded as classics. Author: Italian Fascism, 1934; The French Revolutini (1788-1792), English translation, 1954.

PROFESSIONS

Italian Americans in the various professional fields: medicine, law, engineering, architecture, science and the social sciences.

ARIETI, Silvano

Physician-Neuro Psychiatrist.
Author: Interpretation of Schizophrenia, 1955.
Editor: American Handbook of Psychiatry, 1959.

BELLI, Melvin

Lawyer, born in California, "King of Torts".
Author: Modern Trials and Modern Damages, 6 vol., 1954, Abridged edition, 1962; Ready for the Plaintiff, 1966; Trials and Tort Trends, 14 vols., 1954-1962, etc.

BELLUSCHI, Pietro

Architect - Educator. Dean of Massachusetts Institute of Technology. School of Architecture and Planning, 1951-1965. Appointed by the President as a member of the National Fine Arts Commission, 1950.

CROCCO, Luigi

Physicist, born in Italy; Director of Guggenheim Jet Propulsion Center, Princeton, New Jersey, since 1949. Recipient of the G. Edward Pendray Award, American Rocket Society, 1960.

CUOMO, Mario

Lawyer. Achieved a public image as an advocate espousing the cause of the owners of the Corona houses in Queens County, New York. Recently appointed by Mayor Lindsay as an independent fact-finder in the Forest Hills housing project controversy.

D'AMBROSIO, Richard A.

Clinical Psychologist.
Author: No Other Language but a Cry, 1970.

FINZI, Leo Aldo

Electrical Engineer - Educator, born in Italy. Professor at Carnegie-Mellon University, Pittsburgh, Pennsylvania

119

from 1946 to date. Recipient of the
Carnegie Corporation Award for outstanding teaching, 1955. Author of
numerous technical papers on electrical machinery, magnetic amplifiers,
ferro-magnetism and super conductivity.

FONTANA, Dr. Vincent J.

Physician-Pediatric Allergist.
Physician in attendance for President-
D. Eisenhower, Francis Cardinal Spell-
man, President Nixon, Renata Tebaldi,
and Economist, Arthur Burns. He has
written more than 64 books and articles
on child allergies and child abuse.
Appointed by Mayor Lindsay to the May-
or's Task Force on Child Abuse.

FUBINI, Eugene

Engineer - Business Executive.
Consultant: President's Advisory Com-
mittee, 1957-1961. The U. S. A. F.
Science Advisory Board, 1958 to 1961,
1965 to date.
Received the Presidential Certificate of
Merit, 1956.

GRIMALDI, John Vincent

Safety Engineer - Educator.
Professor, Safety Education at New York
University from 1967 to date.
Author: Control - The Effective Management of Risk, 1966, The Physically Im-
paired - A Guide to their Employment,
1945, etc.

MONTAGNA, William

Scientist, born in Italy.
Assistant Professor, Long Island College of Medicine, New York, 1945 to
1948.
Director: Oregon Regional Primate
Research Center, 1963 to date; recipient
of many awards.
Author: The Epidermis, 1965; co-au-
thored and edited several other related
books.

PINO, Dr. John Anthony

Zoologist - Agricultural scientist.
Director for Agricultural Sciences in
New York, 1970, for the Rockefeller
Foundation.

RASETTI, Franco

Italian Physicist and paleontologist.
Taught at Columbia University, 1935-
1936, Cornell University, 1936; Washington University, 1948 and University
of Miami, 1958. Professor Emeritus
of Physics, Johns Hopkins University,
1958.

ROSSI, Bruno

Italian born American Physicist. Professor of Physics at Massachusetts Institute of Technology from 1966 to date.
He was present at the discovery of slow
neutrons and worked with Enrico Fermi
at Los Alamos.

STOLFI, Dr. Julius E.

Physician.   First Brooklynite to become
Vice-President of the American College
of Physicians, 1972.

VINCENTI, Walter

Aeronautical Engineer.   Aero research
scientist, NACA, 1940 to 1957; Professor of aero and astronautics, Stamford
University, Connecticut from 1957 to
date.
Author (with Charles H. Kruger, Jr.):
Introduction to Physical Gas Dynamics,
1965.

Most Reverend Pius A. Benincasa, D. D.,
>> Diocese of Buffalo, New York,
>> appointed Auxiliary, May 8, 1964.

Most Reverend Joseph B. Brunini, D. D.,
>> Diocese of Natchez–Jackson, Mississip-
>> pi, appointed Ordinary, December 2,
>> 1967.

Most Reverend Anthony G. Bosco, D. D.,
>> Diocese of Pittsburgh, Pennsylvania,
>> appointed Auxiliary, May 14, 1970.

Most Reverend John J. Cassata, D. D.,
>> Diocese of Fort Worth, Texas,
>> appointed Ordinary, August 27, 1969.

Most Reverend Lawrence M. De Falco, D. D.,
>> Diocese of Amarillo, Texas,
>> appointed Ordinary, April 16, 1963.

Most Reverend Charles P. Greco, D. D.,
>> Diocese of Alexandria, Louisiana,
>> appointed Ordinary, January 15, 1946.

Most Reverend Francis J. Mugavero, D. D.,
>> Diocese of Brooklyn, New York,
>> appointed Ordinary, July 17, 1968.

Most Reverend John K. Mussio, D. D.,
>> Diocese of Steubenville, Ohio,
>> appointed Ordinary, March 16, 1945.

Most Reverend Joseph M. Pernicone, D. D.,
>> Archidiocese of New York,
>> appointed Auxiliary, April 6, 1954.

Most Reverend Celestine Joseph Damiano, D. D.,
>> Dioces of Camden, New Jersey,
>> Died October, 1967.

AUTO RACING

Some prominent Italian Americans in Auto Racing are:

ANDRETTI, Mario	U. S. A. C.* National Champion; 1966 - Drove the fastest single lap in the history of racing, 164.1 miles per hour. 1969 - Winner of the Indianapolis "500". 1971 - Winner of the World Drivers Championship Series.
ASCARI, Alberto	1952-1953 World Sports Car Racing Champion.
DE PALMA, Ralph	Uncle and trainer of Peter De Paolo. 1915 - Winner of the Indianapolis "500".
DE PAOLO, Peter	The first to break the 100 miles per hour mark. 1925 - Winner of the Indianapolis "500".
FARINA, Giuseppe	1950 World Sports Car Racing Champion.
GRANATELLI, Andy	Avid promoter and designer of racing cars; his brother, Vince, is usually crew chief.

*The abbreviation U.S.A.C. stands for the United States Auto Club, Indianapolis, Indiana; the scene of the famous "500" race under the auspices of the U.S.A.C.

BASEBALL

There must be an affinity between Italians and baseball since so many of them have done so well.

Especially colorful and high in achievement were:

ANTONELLI, Johnny   New York, National League. 1954 pitcher with best won/lost percentage, won 21, lost 7, .750%

BERRA, Yogi   New York, American League. Voted the Most Valuable Player Award in 1951, 1954 and 1955. One of the home run greats with 358 Home Run total. Made Manager of the New York Mets, 1972.

CAVARETTA, Phil   Chicago, National League. Played a record 22 seasons and 2,475 games. National League Batting Champion in 1945 with a .355 average. Most Valuable Player Award for 1945.

CAMILLI, Dolph   Brooklyn, National League. Runs-Batted-in Leader for 1941 with 120 RBI; Home-run champion for 1941 with 34 Home Runs; Voted Most Valuable Player Award for 1941.

COLAVITO, Rocky   Cleveland, American League. Runs-Batted-in Leader for 1965 with 108 RBI; Home Run Champion for 1959 with 42 Home Runs. Home Run Leader with 374 Home Run total.

CROSETTI, Frank   New York, American League. Active in baseball as a player and coach from 1932 to 1968. He played and coached 23 World Series games.

ASPROMONTE, Ken   Named manager of the Cleveland Indians, Winter 1971; prior to that Ken was a "utility player", for eight years, with six different clubs.

CONIGLIARO, Tony

Boston, American League.
Home Run Champion for 1965 with 32
Home Runs.

DI MAGGIO, Joe

New York, American League.
Elected to the Baseball Hall of Fame -
1955.   (See Chronology).

FURILLO, Carl

Brooklyn, National League.   Batting
Champion for 1953 with a .344 average.

LAZZERI, Tony

New York, American League.   One of
Murderers' Row, the famous line-up of
Yankee hitters from 1926 to 1929.
One of the few players to hit a home-run
with bases loaded in a World Series
Game.

LOMBARDI, Ernie

Cincinnati, National League.
Batting Champion for 1938 and 1942 with
.342 and .330 average respectively.
Most Valuable Player Award for 1938.

RASCHI, Vic

New York, American League.
1950 Pitcher with best won/lost percentage; won 21, lost 8, .724%.

RIZZUTO, Phil

New York, American League.   Most
Valuable Player Award for 1950.
CBS Sportscaster.

ITALIAN AMERICANS IN THE AMERICAN LEAGUE ROSTER

(Start of the 1971 Season)

Name	Position	Team
CONIGLIARO, Billy	OF	Boston Red Sox
FIORE, Mike	1B-OF	Boston Red Sox
GAGLIANO, Phil	INF	Boston Red Sox
PETROCELLI, Rico	3B-SS	Boston Red Sox
CONIGLIARO, Tony	OF	California Angels
FREGOSI, Jim	SS	California Angels
CAMILLI, Lou	3B	Cleveland Indians
MINGORI, Steve	P	Cleveland Indians
CAMPISI, Sal	P	Minnesota Twins
TEPEDINO, Frank	1B-OF	New York Yankees
LA RUSSA, Tony	2B	Oakland Athletics
RUDI, Joe	OF-1B	Oakland Athletics

ITALIAN AMERICANS IN THE NATIONAL LEAGUE ROSTER

(Start of the 1971 Season)

Name	Position	Team
PEPITONE, Joe	OF-1B	Chicago Cubs
BOCCABELLA, John	C-1B	Montreal Espos
ASPROMONTE, Bob	3B	New York Mets
FRISELLA, Danny	P	New York Mets
GIUSTI, Dave	P	Pittsburgh Pirates
TORRE, Joe	3B-1B	St. Louis Cardinals
CANNIZZARO, Chris	C	San Diego Padres
FERRARA, Al	OF	San Diego Padres
SANTORINI, Al	P	San Diego Padres
SPIEZIO, Ed	3B	San Diego Padres

BASKETBALL

The basketball court is the arena of tall men. Some there are who have capitalized on their speed and smaller stature; but these are few. The Italian concentration, therefore, is admittedly limited in this field.

LAVELLI, Tony — Set the all-time record as college scoring champion for 1949: 30 games, 671 points. (Yale University).

LUISETTI, Angelo "Hank" — One of basketball's most sensational players who revolutionized the game by making one-hand shots while running at top speed. In the Stamford-LIU game of December 30, 1936, "Hank" out-passed, out-shot, out-raced every LIU player. All American - four times; College Player of the year - twice.

MELCHIONI, Bill — New York Nets, ABA League. During 1971/72 Bill Melchioni led the league in assists; averages about nine assists per game.

RINALDI, Rick — Individual scoring leader in the Major Colleges for 1970/71, with 24 games and 687 points.

COACHES

BIANCHI, Al — Virginia Squires (Eastern Division of the ABA)

CARNESECCA, Lou — New York Nets (Eastern Division of the ABA)

BOWLING

Bowling, in its earlier decades, was practically an Italian American sport; most of its prominent names at that time were Italian. More recently, however, the appeal of the sport has spread to every group and now it's everybody's game.

ELECTED TO THE
AMERICAN BOWLING CONGRESS *
HALL OF FAME

NAME	YEAR
CAMPI, Lou	1968
CASSIO, Marty	1972
FARAGALLI, Al	1968
FAZIO, Basil (Buzz)	1963
MARINO, Hank	1941
MARTINO, John	1969
MERCURIO, Walter	1967
SMITH, Jimmy (nee MELLILO)	1941(Charter member)
SPERANDO, Tony	1968
SPINELLA, Barney	1968
VARIPAPA, Andy	1957

*Members are elected by the Bowling Writers' Association of America. The writer must have at least ten years experience in covering bowling events. Players must bowl for twenty years in national tournaments to be elegible and must receive 75% of the writers' votes to be elected.

The following names are just a few of the many other Italian Americans with prominent bowling records:

FALCARO, Joe — One of the sport's most popular players. Proficient as a "head to head" bowler.

LIMONGELLO, Mike — 1965 winner of the Professional Bowlers Association Tournament held in Sacramento, California.
Former National Professional Champion and U. S. Open Champion.

MARTORELLA, Millie — Three time Women's International Bowling Congress Queens Championship.

NOTARO, Phyllis — 1961 Woman Champion of the All-Star Tournament of the Bowling Proprietors Association of America.

SALVINO, Carmine — One of the top professional bowlers; holds more than ten professional titles. Won the Professional Bowling Association of America Tournament in 1964 in Jacksonville, Florida, in 1964 in Rockford, Illinois and in 1961 in Albany, New York.

SANTORE, Frank — Won the singles title and the all-events title in the American Bowling Congress Championship Tournament in 1950 and the all-events title in the same tournament held in 1952.

PETRAGLIA, John — Winner of more than $85,000.00 in tournaments played during the year 1971. John is 24 years old.

BOXING

The "ring" has attracted many of the sons of Italy in America, and many entered its halls of fame. Here are just a few of the many who reached the elusive heights of championship:

BASILIO, Carmen

1955 to 1956 - Welterweight Champion.
1957 to 1958 - Middleweight Champion.
1955 and 1957 - Recipient of the Edward J. Neil Trophy award.

BARBELLA, Rocco
(known as ROCKY GRAZIANO)

1947 to 1948 - Middleweight Champion.

BERNARDINELLI, Giuseppe
ANTONIO
(known as JOEY MAXIM)

1950 to 1952 - Light-heavyweight Champion.

CANZONERI, Tony

1930 to 1933 - Lightweight Champion.
1956 - Elected to the Hall of Fame.

DE MARCO, Paddy

1954 - Lightweight Champion

DE MARCO, Tony

1955 - Welterweight Champion

DUNDEE, Joe

1927 to 1929 - Welterweight Champion.

GALENTO, Tony

Contender for the heavyweight championship; 1939 - fought and lost to Joe Louis.
Affectionately known as "Two-Ton Tony".

HAYES, Petey
(ne Mancuso)

1921-Winner of the New York State National Guard Junior Lightweight title; 1923-Winner of the New York State National Guard Lightweight title.
Product of the lower east side (New York), known as "Old Lion Heart". Retired in 1926 after 125 fights.

GIARDELLO, Joey

1963 to 1965 - Middleweight Champion.

LA MOTTA, Jake

1949 to 1951 - Middleweight Champion.

NOVA, Lou

Contender for the heavyweight championship; 1941 - fought and lost to Joe Louis.

131

PEP, Willie   1942 to 1948 - Featherweight Champion.
(nee PAPALEO)   1949 - Regained the title and held it un-
                               til 1950.
                               1963-Elected to the Boxing Hall of Fame.

PETROLLE, Billy   1962-Elected to the Boxing Hall of Fame.

SALICA, Lou   1935- Bantamweight Champion.
                               1940 - Regained the title until 1942.

FOOTBALL

Among the many Italian-American men of fame in the rugged sport of pigskin and gridiron, a representative few are mentioned here.

AMECHE, Alan
1954-Heisman Memorial Trophy Winner;
Team: Wisconsin University
1955-National Football League Star Rusher.

BELLINO, Joe
1960-Heisman Memorial Trophy winner;
Team: Navy.

BERTELLI, Angelo
1943-Heisman Memorial Trophy winner;
Team: Notre Dame University.

CAPPELLETTI, Gino
American Football League Scoring Champion in 1961, 1963 and 1964.

DE PRATO, John
1915 - College Scoring Champion;
Team: Michigan State University.

LAMONICA, Daryle
1967 - American Football League Star Passer. Record All-Time Great AFL Passer for seven years, through the 1969 football season.
Often referred to as the "Babe Ruth" of football.

MARCHETTI, Gino
Elected to the Professional Football Hall of Fame in 1972.

MARINARO, Ed
1971-Heisman Memorial Trophy winner;
Team: Cornell University.

MORABITO, Anthony J. and
MORABITO, Vincent P.,
Brothers.
Founded the San Francisco 49ers in 1945.

NOMELLINI, Leo
Elected to the Professional Football Hall of Fame.
Played tackle for the San Francisco 49ers from 1950 to 1963.

PARILLI, Babe
Record All-Time Great AFL Passer for ten years, through the 1969 football season.

133

PATERNO, Joe

1968-College Football Coach of the Year award.   Team.   Penn State University.

PICCOLO, Brian

1964-College Scoring Champion; Team: Wake Forest University Played halfback for the Chicago Bears. Died of cancer at age 26 on June 16, 1970 in New York City.

ROBUSTELLI, Andy

Elected to the Professional Football Hall of Fame. Played Defensive end with the Los Angeles Rams from 1951 to 1955 and with the New York Giants from 1956 to 1964.

SPADIA, Lou

President of the San Francisco 49ers.

TRIPPI, Charles

Elected to the College Football Hall of Fame in 1945 and 1946; Team: Georgia Tech.

GOLF

Representative names, but not exhaustive of the many Italian-Americans with high achievement in golf, are the following:

CAPONI, Donna

U. S. Golf Association Women's Open Golf Championship winner in 1969 and 1970.

GAGLIARDI, Joseph P.

1951 Runner-up in the U.S. Golf Association's Amateur Golf Championship.

GHEZZI, Vic

Elected to the Professional Golfers Association's Hall of Fame.
1941 winner of the PGA title.

SARAZEN, Gene
(nee SARACENI, Eugene)

1935 - Double Eagle Shot in the Masters Tournament;
1932 - Winner of both the U. S. and British Opens in the same year;
1922 - Won both the U. S. Open and PGA title in the same year.

STRAFACI, Frankie

Holds the record for winning the Metropolitan Golf Association Amateur Championship seven times; in 1938, 1939, 1945, 1946, 1947, 1950 and 1954.

URZETTA, Sam

1950 winner in the U. S. Golf Association's Amateur Golf Championship.

VENTURI, Ken

Winner in the -
1964 - /U. S. Open Golf Championship.

SOME REPRESENTATIVE ITALIAN NEWSPAPERS & PERIODICALS

BY STATE

Connecticut

    Rowayton. Italian Heritage, monthly.

California

    Los Angeles. L'Italo-Americano, weekly.

    San Francisco. Bollettino

    Santa Barbara. Italica, quarterly.

    Riverside. Italian Quarterly, quarterly.

Illinois

    Chicago. Fra Noi, monthly.

    La Parola del Popolo, monthly.

Massachusetts

    Boston. Post Gazette, weekly.

    Sons of Italy News, monthly.

Michigan

    Dearborn. Il Mondo Libero, monthly.

    Detroit. Italian Tribune of America, weekly.

New Jersey

    Atlantic City. Il Popolo Italiano, monthly.

    Bloomfield. Unico National Magazine, monthly.

    Newark. Italian Tribune News, weekly.

    Trenton. La Nuova Capitale, monthly.

New York

  Bronx: Italo American Times, monthly.

  Brooklyn: Il Crociato, weekly.

           Italian American Review, irregular

           Italian Historical Society, irregular

           The National Italian American News, bi-monthly.

  Buffalo: Forum Italicum, quarterly.

  Elmhurst: Italian Charities of America, monthly.

  New York City: ACIM Dispatch (American Committee on Italian Migration), monthly.

           American Review of Art and Science, bi-monthly.

           Il Progresso Italo-Americano, daily.

           Italamerican, monthly.

           Italian Scene, irregular.

           La Follia di New York, monthly.

           L'Adunato dei Refrattari, monthly.

           Newsletter, (Istituto Italiano di Cultura), bi-monthly.

           The Challenge, monthly.

           Voce Libertaria, monthly.

  Staten Island: International Migration Review, quarterly.

Pennsylvania

  Philadelphia: National Sons of Italy, weekly.

           Times, (Sons of Italy), weekly.

Rhode Island

      Providence: The Echo, weekly.

The following magazines are published in Italy but enjoy a substantial
circulation in the United States:

                            Oggi
                            L'Europeo
                            Annabella
                            Novella
                            Il Mondo

The following materials are available, free of charge, to libraries, schools and teachers, from the Institute of Italian Culture, 686 Park Avenue, New York, N. Y. 10021.

BOOKLETS:
    Italy (General Information for Travelers) (48 p.)

    Summer Courses in Italy (37 p.)

CATALOGS (limited supply):

    Educational Films and Audiovisual Aids from the Institute's Collection (1971-1972) (24 p.)

    List (1968) of 16 mm. Italian Feature Films available from commercial distributors in the U. S. A.
    Appendix (1970) (18 p.)

FACTS ABOUT ITALY:

    Women in Italy

    Folk Dances (in preparation)

    Folk Costumes (in preparation)

    The Italians and their Food (in preparation)

    Folkways and Festivals (in preparation)

OCCASIONAL PAPERS (average 1 to 4 pages):

    Employment Possibilities for American Teachers in Italy.

    Short Term Employment in Italy.

    Long Term Residence and Employment Possibilities in Italy for American Citizens.

    Rules for Admission of Foreign Students to Italian Universities.

    Education in Italy.

    Suggested List of Schools in Italy for English-speaking Students.

BIBLIOGRAPHY

General Reference Materials

Cordasco, Francesco and La Gumina, Salvatore. Italians in the United States. New York: Oriole Editions, 1972.

>By far the most comprehensive, practical, up-to-date and available source for reports, texts, critical studies and related materials about Italians in America. The general introduction and headnotes preceeding each section are careful, evaluative guides to the literature introduced thereunder. (The Cordasco-La Gumina and De Conde (supra) comments should be carefully read before entering upon any serious study of the sources pertaining to the Italians in America.)

The New York Times. Encyclopedic Almanac 1972. New York, N. Y.

Immigration & Naturalization Service. 1970 Annual Report. Washington, D.C.: U. S. Government Printing Office, 1970.

Schiavo, Giovanni, ed. Italian-American Who's Who. (vol. XIX) New York: Vigo Press, 1962-1963.

Velikonja, Joseph. Italians in the United States. Occasional Papers No. 1. Department of Geography, Southern Illinois University, Carbondale, Illinois: 1963.
>(A pioneer in the compilation of bibliography on Italian-Americans.)

Popular Materials

Federal Writers' Project. The Italians of New York. N. Y.: Random House, 1938.

Fermi, Laura. Atoms in the Family. Chicago: The University of Chicago Press, 1954.

Garlick, Richard C., Jr. et al. Italy and Italians in Washington's Time. New York: Italian Publishers, 1933.

Glazer, Nathan and Daniel P. Moynihan. Beyond the Melting Pot. 2nd ed. Cambridge: M.I.T. Press, 1970.

Grossman, Ronald P. The Italians in America. Minneapolis: Lerner Publications, 1966.

Iorizzo, Luciano J. and Mondello Salvatore. The Italian-Americans. New York: Twayne Publishers, Inc., 1971.

141

Josephson, Matthew and Hannah. Al Smith: Hero of the Cities. Boston: Houghton Mifflin Company, 1969.

La Gumina, Salvatore J. Vito Marcantonio: The People's Politician, Dubuque: Kendal/Hunt Publishing Company, 1969.

Lopreato, Joseph. The Italian Americans. New York: Random House, 1970.

Lorit, Sergio C. Frances Cabrini. New York and London: New York City Press, 1970.

Lord, Elliot, John D. Trenner, Samuel Barrows. The Italian in America. New York: B. F. Buck and Company, 1906. Reprinted, San Francisco: R. & E. Research Associates, 1970.

Marinacci, Barbara. They Came from Italy. New York: Dodd, Mead and Company, 1967.

McFadden, Elizabeth. The Glitter and the Gold. Dial Press, New York, 1971.
    (A spirited account of the Metropolitan Museum of Art's first Director,
        Luigi Palma Di Cesnola.)

Morison, Samuel Eliot. Admiral of the Ocean Sea. Boston: Atlantic Monthly Press, 1942.
(Condensed version of the scholarly work by Morison bearing same title.)

Musmanno, Michael A. The Italians in America. Garden City, New York: Doubleday and Company, Inc. 1965.

Novak, Michael. The Rise of the Unmeltable Ethnics. The MacMillan Co., New York, 1972.

Rolle, Andrew F. The Immigrant Upraised: Italian Adventurers and Colonists in an Expanding America. Norman, Oklahoma: University of Oklahoma Press, 1968.

Russell, Francis. Tragedy in Dedham. New York: McGraw Hill, 1962. (The Sacco-Vanzetti Case).

Schiavo, Giovanni Ermenigildo. Italians in America Before the Civil War. New York: G. P. Putnam's Sons, 1924. (2nd ed. 1934).
Four Centuries of Italian-American History. New York: Vigo Press, 1952. (2nd and 3rd eds.)
Italian-American History. (2 vols.) New York: Vigo Press, 1947 - 1949.

Scholarly Materials

Cammett, John M., ed. The Italian American Novel. New York: American Italian Historical Association, 1969.
(Proceedings of a symposium).

Campisi, Paul J. "Ethnic Family Patterns: The Italian Family in the
United States," American Journal of Sociology v. 53 (May, 1948), pp. 443-
449.

   Also published as, "The Italian Family in the United States,"   Milton
   L. Barron, American Minorities. New York: Alfred Knopf, 1957.

Child, Irvin Long. Italian or American? The Second Generation in
Conflict. New Haven: Yale University Press, 1943.

   Reissued with introduction by F. Cordasco, New York: Russell &
   Russell, 1970. [Originally, Ph.D. dissertation, Yale University,
   1939.]

De Conde, Alexander. Half Bitter, Half Sweet. New York: Charles
Scribner's Sons, 1971.
   (Offers an incisive evaluation of the various sources to which he re-
   fers.)

Iorizzo, Luciano J., ed. An Inquiry into Organized Crime. New York:
American Italian Historical Association, 1970. (   )
(Proceedings of a symposium).

La Gumina, Salvatore, ed. Ethnicity in American Political Life. The
Italian American Experience. New York: American Italian Historical
Association, 1968. (   )
(Proceedings of a symposium).

Mazzei, Philip. Memoirs. Trans. by H. R. Marraro. New York:
Columbia University Press, 1942.

Morison, Samuel Eliot. The European Discovery of America. Philadelphia: Oxford University Press, 1971. Admiral of the Ocean Sea. (2 vols.)
Boston: Little, Brown and Co. for Atlantic Monthly Press, 1942.

Segre, Emilio. Enrico Fermi/Scientist. Chicago and London: The University Press, 1970.

Seltsam, William H. Metropolitan Opera Annals - Second Supplement,
1957-1966. New York: The H. W. Wilson Company, 1968.

Tomasi, Lidio F., ed. The Italians in America, The Progressive View, 1891-1914. New York: Center for Migration Studies, 1972.

Tomasi, Silvano M. and Engel, Madeline H., eds. The Italian Experience in the United States. Staten Island, New York: Center for Migration Studies, 1970.

Tomasi, Silvano M., ed. International Migration Review, vol. 1, No. 3 Staten Island, New York: Center for Migration Studies, Summer, 1967. (Issue devoted to Italian-American Experience.)

Vespucci, Amerigo. Letter to Piero Soderini, 1504. Trans. by George Tyler Northup. New Jersey: Princeton University Press, 1916.

Wroth, Lawrence C. The Voyages of Giovanni da Verrazzano 1524-1528. New Haven and London: Yale University Press, 1970.

Unpublished Works

Fenten, Edwin. Immigrants and Unions, A Case Study: Italians and American Labor, 1870-1920. Unpublished doctoral thesis, Harvard University, 1957.

Gallo, Patrick J. Political Alienation Among Italians of the New York Metropolitan Region. Unpublished doctoral thesis, New York University, 1971.

Giannotta, Rosario O. Contributions of Italians to the Development of American Culture during the Eighteenth Century. Unpublished doctoral thesis, St. John's University, 1942.

Piccinni, Gaetano. Blessed Frances Xavier Cabrini in America. [Unpublished M. A. thesis, Columbia University, 1942.]

Matthews, Sr. Mary Fabian. The Role of the Public Schools in the Assimilation of the Italian Immigrant Child in New York City 1900-1914. Unpublished doctoral thesis, Fordham University, 1966.

McLaughlin, Virginia. Like the Fingers of the Hand: The Family and Common Life of First Generation Italian Americans in Buffalo, New York, 1880-1930. Unpublished doctoral thesis, University of New York in Buffalo, 1970.

Mondello, Salvatore Alfred. The Italian Immigrant in Urban America, 180-1920, as reported in the contemporary periodical press. Unpublished doctoral thesis, New York University, 1960.

Peebles, Robert. Leonard Covello: An Immigrant's Contribution to New York City. Unpublished doctoral thesis, New York University, 1967.

Russo, Nicholas. The Religious Acculturation of the Italians in New York City. Unpublished doctoral thesis, St. John's University, 1968.

Sandalls, Kathrine F. An Investigation of the Differential of Fertility Patterns of Irish and Italian Americans. [Unpublished M. A. thesis, Georgetown University, 1970] .

Smith, William Barry. The Attitudes of Catholic Americans toward Italian Fascism between the two World Wars. Unpublished doctoral thesis, Catholic University of America, 1969.

Tomasi, Silvano M. Assimilation and Religion: The Role of the Italian Ethnic Church in the New York Metropolitan Area, 1880-1930. Unpublished doctoral thesis, Fordham University, 1972.

Valletta, Clement L. A Study of Americanization in Carneta: Italian American Identity through Three Generations. Unpublished doctoral thesis, University of Pennsylvania, 1968.

Vecoli, Rudolph J. Chicago's Italians Prior to World War I: A Study of their Social and Economic adjustment. Unpublished doctoral thesis, University of Wisconsin, 1963.

INDEX

147